Merry Christmas and Happy New Year

Arnold R. Schaffer
Chief Executive

Providence Health System
San Fernando and
Santa Clarita Valleys Service Area

Providence | Health System

The Art of **HEALING**

Doctors

Jokes, Quotes, and Anecdotes

Doctors

Jokes, Quotes, and Anecdotes

BARNES
&NOBLE
BOOKS
NEW YORK

Cover illustration by Tom Patrick
Illustrations by Kevin Brimmer

Nothing is more fatal to health than overcare of it.

—Benjamin Franklin

◆

Just once I'd like to say to that doctor, "You know, I'm not ready for you yet. Why don't you go back in that little office and I'll be with you in a moment. And get your pants off."

—Jerry Seinfeld

Introduction

Benjamin Franklin penned the witticism on the previous page in the mid-1700s. Jerry Seinfeld's quip is circa late-20th century. The times may change, but doctor jokes will always be around.

Why do we so love to make fun of doctors? Is it their propensity for swollen egos, the long waiting room stays, the poking and prodding of otherwise private bodily areas, the row of BMWs in the hospital parking lot? Hey, pick a reason—they're all great!

Maybe it's because on the day we're born, a doctor welcomes us into the world with a slap on the behind—and a doctor most likely will be helping to usher us out of the world too, when that dark day finally comes.

Whatever the reason, poking fun at doctors has been a favorite pastime since Hippocrates first took his oath. This book presents some of history's very best one-liners, clever quotes, and jokes concerning the noble profession of medicine and its practitioners. And, because truth is often stranger—and funnier—than fiction, there's also plenty of fact-based fun, like:

Medical chart bloopers: "Patient complaining of headache. Tylenol given as ordered. Checked back with pt one hour later and head gone."

Strange but true phobias: Peladophobia: The fear of bald people. Pupaphobia: The fear of puppets.

Real illnesses and their actual medical names: Humper's Lump: Swelling suffered by hotel porters from lugging heavy bags.

Excerpts from medical memos: "Cardiac patients should not be referred to with MUH (messed-up heart), PBS (pretty bad shape), PCL (pre-code looking), or HIBGIA (had it before, got it again).

Unless you've had your funny bone surgically removed, you're sure to find something in this book to chuckle at—even if your name happens to be followed by the initials M.D. Hey, no matter what doctors say, laughter is still the best medicine… so let the healing begin.

—Patrick Regan

How can you tell when a surgeon's
mind is wandering?

Before he makes an incision, he yells, "Fore!"

◆

STRANGE BUT TRUE MEDICAL STORIES

A father called his son's pediatrician, very upset because he had caught the boy eating ants. The doctor reassured him that ants are not harmful and there would be no need to bring the child into the hospital.

The father was much relieved and ended the conversation by saying, "Guess I didn't need to give him that ant poison then, but better safe than sorry." The doctor told the man that he had better bring the boy to the ER right away.

A group of doctors was seated together for lunch at an international conference. Each seemed eager to impress his colleagues. First the Israeli doctor said, "Medicine in my country is so advanced that we can take a kidney out of one man, put it in another, and have him looking for work in six weeks."

Then the German doctor said, "That is nothing. We can take a lung out of one person, put it in another, and have him looking for work in four weeks."

Then the Russian doctor said, "In my country, medicine is so advanced that we can take half a heart out of one person, put it in another, and have them both looking for work in two weeks."

Finally the American doctor, not to be outdone, said, "You guys are way behind. We took a man with no brain out of Texas, put him in the White House, and now half the country is looking for work."

"I'm giving you a prescription to help you lose weight," the doctor told the patient, "but for it to work, you must follow my instructions precisely."

"Of course," said the patient.

"Every morning, take the bottle of 300 pills, pour them onto the floor, and pick them up, one by one."

◆

A Russian cosmonaut has an emergency during his reentry into Earth's atmosphere, and his spacecraft crash-lands in the Australian bush. When he comes to consciousness, he finds himself in a bush medical clinic, bandaged from head to toe. Standing at the side of his cot is a tough and tanned Aussie doctor.

"Did I come here to die?" the cosmonaut asks gravely.

"No, mate," the doctor replies, "ya came here yestadie ..."

A general practitioner and a nurse were on the train, going to a medical conference. Opposite them was a man furiously scratching his elbow.

"I wonder what's the matter with him?" said the nurse.

"He's a patient of mine," the doctor replied, "and, in confidence, I can tell you that he suffers badly from hemorrhoids."

"Well, why is he scratching there, then?"

"Oh, he's a politician. He doesn't know his ass from his elbow."

MEMO
To: Medical Personnel
From: Human Resources

It has come to our attention from several emergency rooms that many EMS narratives have taken a decidedly creative direction lately. Effective immediately, all members are to refrain from using slang and abbreviations to describe patients, such as the following:

• Cardiac patients should not be referred to with MUH (messed-up heart), PBS (pretty bad shape), PCL (pre-code looking), or HIBGIA (had it before, got it again).

• Trauma patients are not FDGB (fall down, go boom), TBC (total body crunch), or HH (hamburger helper).

*I had a rough childhood. When I was born,
the doctor advised me of my rights.*

—Scott Roeben

◆

A high school student is in the counselor's office.

"So, what things interest you?"

"I'd like to cut people open and run my fingers through their intestines!"

There's a long pause. The counselor makes a half-hearted chuckle and says, "Well, I guess that means you'll either be a surgeon or a psychotic killer. Tell me a little more about yourself."

"Well, to start with, I'm never wrong," the student says. "Other people worship me and do exactly as I say—or if they don't, they should."

The counselor brightens. "Surgeon it is!"

IT'S A FACT

In 2002, a study by the Joint Commission on Accreditation of Healthcare Organizations found that almost one-quarter of all unanticipated patient deaths and complications result from a shortage of nurses. The study examined over 1,600 patient deaths and injuries and found that low nursing staff levels were a contributing factor in 24 percent of the cases.

A man went to the doctor complaining of insomnia. The doctor gave him an exam and found nothing physically wrong with him.

"Listen," the doctor said, "if you ever expect to cure your insomnia, you need to stop taking your troubles to bed with you."

"It's true," said the man, "but my wife refuses to sleep alone."

CAFFEINE IS MY SHEPHERD

Caffeine is my shepherd; I shall not doze.

It maketh me to wake in the lecture hall,

It leadeth me beyond the sleeping masses.

It restoreth my buzz.

*It leadeth me in the paths of consciousness
for its name's sake.*

*Yea, though I walk through the
valley of the shadow of addiction,*

I will fear no decaf,

*For thou art with me.
Thy cream and thy sugar, they comfort me.*

*Thou preparest a tall latte before me in the
presence of fatigue.*

Thou anointest my day with pep; my mug runneth over.

*Surely richness and taste shall follow me all the days of
my life, and I will dwell in the House of Java forever.*

—Anonymous

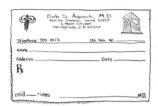

At an international conference, an American, a Brit, and a Russian were discussing the shortcomings of their diagnoses.

"I can't stand it sometimes," said the American. "We treat people for cancer, and then they die of AIDS."

"I know what you mean," said the Brit. "We treat them for yellow fever, and it turns out they had malaria."

"That is not a problem in our country," said the Russian doctor. "When we treat people for a disease, they die of that disease."

First the doctor told me the good news: I was going to have a disease named after me.

—Steve Martin

◆

STRANGE BUT TRUE PHOBIAS

- Aulophobia is the fear of flutes.

- Nephophobia is the fear of clouds.

- Xanthophobia is the fear of the color yellow.

A young man was feeling ill, so he asked a friend to recommend an internist. "I know a great one," the friend said, "but he's very expensive. He charges $400 for the first visit and $100 for each visit after that."

The man went to see the doctor. Trying to save money, he greeted the doctor when he entered the exam room with a boisterous, "I'm back!"

The doctor proceeded with the examination. "Very good," he said when he was finished. "Just continue the treatment I prescribed last time."

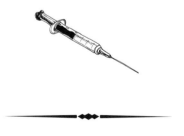

An eighty-three-year-old lady finished her annual physical examination, whereupon the doctor said, "You are in fine shape for your age . . . but tell me . . . do you still have intercourse?"

"Just a minute," she said. "I'll have to ask my husband." She went out to the reception room and said, "Jake, do we still have intercourse?"

The husband turned blue in the face and answered, "If I told you once I told you a thousand times: We have Blue Cross!"

The optometrist pointed to the top of the eye chart and said, "Now read this."

"I'm sorry, you'll have to read it to me," the patient replied. "Didn't anybody tell you I was here on account of my poor eyesight?"

◆

How does Michael Jackson pick his nose?

He looks through a catalog in
the plastic surgeon's office.

*The trouble with being a hypochondriac these days is
that antibiotics have cured all the good diseases.*

—Caskie Stinnett

You've Been an ER Doctor Too Long If . . .

• your idea of comforting a child involves using a papoose board.

• you assume every patient with back pain is a drug-seeker until proven otherwise.

• you find yourself telling the Motrin overdose which of her medicines are really dangerous.

◆

While visiting a friend who was in the hospital, a man noticed several pretty nurses, each of whom was wearing a pin designed to look like an apple. "What does the pin signify?" he asked one of them.

"Nothing," she said with a smile. "We just use it to keep the doctors away."

TV MEDICINE

Dr. Cox: Well gosh, I guess I became a doctor because ever since I was a little boy I just wanted to help people. I don't tell this story often, but I remember when I was seven years old, one time I found a bird that had fallen out of its nest, and so I picked him up and I brought him home, and I made him a house out of an empty shoebox. [Starts laughing.] I became a doctor for the same four reasons that everybody does: chicks, money, power, and chicks.

—Scrubs

The head doctor at the psychiatric hospital was examining a patient to see if she was ready to reenter society.

"So, Ms. Clark," the doctor said, "I see by your chart that you've been recommended for dismissal. Do you have any idea what you might do once you're released?"

The patient thought for a moment. "Well," she replied, "I studied mechanical engineering, and that's a good field. On the other hand, I might return to school to prepare for a new career. Engineering is still dominated by men."

"I'm not so sure," the doctor said. "I know several successful female engineers."

"Female? No no, I'm not talking about sex discrimination. I'm talking about discrimination against cabbages!"

An eighth-grade teacher was leading a discussion on the qualifications for being president of the United States. After the teacher commented that a person must be a natural-born citizen, one of the students raised her hand. "Does that mean that if you were born by Caesarean section that you can't be president?"

The best doctor is the one you run for
and can't find.

—Denis Diderot

A man went to his first proctological exam. The nurse told him to have a seat in the well air-conditioned examination room and that the doctor would be with him in just a few minutes. As he waited, he noticed that there were three items on a stand next to the doctor's desk: a tube of K-Y jelly, a rubber glove, and a beer.

When the doctor appeared, the man said, "Look Doc, this is my first exam. I know what the K-Y is for, and I know what the glove is for, but what's the beer for?" The doctor cursed in exasperation, flung open the door, and yelled to his nurse, "Nurse! I said to bring me a butt light!"

◆

A standard question on many hospital admission forms, designed to assess a patient's orientation, is "Where are you now?"

Many times the patient writes, "I'm right here!"

TV MEDICINE

Dr. Cox: I became a doctor for the same four reasons everybody does: Chicks, money, power, and chicks. But, since HMOs have made it virtually impossible to make any real money, which directly affects the number of chicks who come sniffing around—and don't ask me what tree they're barkin' up, 'cause they're sure as hell not pissin' on mine. And as far as power goes, well, here I am during my free time letting some thirteen-year-old psychology fellow who couldn't cut it in real medicine ask me questions about my personal life. So, here's the inside scoop, there, pumpkin: Why don't you go ahead and tell me all about power.

—Scrubs

There is a knock on the pearly gates. Saint Peter looks out, and a man is standing there. Saint Peter is about to begin his interview when the man disappears.

A moment later there's another knock. Saint Peter gets the door, sees the man, opens his mouth to speak, but the man disappears once again.

"Hey, are you playing games with me?" Saint Peter calls after him, annoyed.

"No," the man's distant voice replies anxiously. "They're trying to resuscitate me."

A psychologist is in a group meeting with four women and their children. He tells the mothers that they each have an obsessive disorder. Astonished, the mothers become angry with the doctor, wanting to know why he would say such a thing. The doctor calmly begins to explain, "Ma'am, you're obsessed with alcohol, and you named your daughter Brandy."

Then he says to the second mother, "You have an eating disorder, and you named your daughter Candy."

To the third mother he explains, "You're obsessed with money, so you named your daughter Penny."

Before the doctor could tell the fourth mother what she was obsessed with, she whispers to her son, "Come on, Richard, let's go."

It's no longer a question of staying healthy. It's a question of finding a sickness you like.

—Jackie Mason

◆

You've Been an ER Doctor Too Long If . . .

• you've told a crying drunken driver that God was trying to kill him, but God missed.

• you consider yourself a specialist in vague symptoms of long duration.

• you believe patients taking two or more psychiatric drugs will never have real pathology.

• you've forgotten that "vegetable" is a food group.

On the hospital radio the DJ was reading out a request. "This is a special birthday dedication to Sarah, who's one hundred and eleven!"

Amazed that someone could be so old, he looked again at the note in front of him, then cleared his throat and said, "Disregard that last request. This one's a special birthday dedication to Sarah, who's ill."

TV MEDICINE

Hospital Chairman: Dr. Nick, this malpractice committee has received a few complaints against you. Of the 160 gravest charges, the most troubling are performing major operations with a knife and fork from a seafood restaurant.

—The Simpsons

The pope, an HMO CEO, and a medical student are flying on an airplane. The captain comes back and says that he has some bad news and some really bad news. "The bad news," he tells them, "is that the plane is going to crash." He puts on a parachute and just before jumping says, "The really bad news is that there are only two more parachutes."

"I'm one of the smartest men in the world," the HMO CEO says. "Without me, there would be no healthcare system as we now know it." He then puts on a parachute and jumps.

"Well, my child," the pope says, "I would love to live, but I believe that my time is up. Please take the other parachute."

"Not to worry, Your Holiness," the medical student says. "Right now one of the smartest men in the world is looking for the rip-cord on my backpack."

Four Ways to Know You Joined a Cheap HMO

1. Tongue depressors taste of Fudgsicle.

2. Annual breast exams are conducted at Hooters.

3. You swear you saw salad tongs and a crab fork on the instrument tray just before the anesthesia kicked in.

4. You ask for Viagra. You get a Fudgsicle stick and duct tape.

Middle age is the time when a man is always thinking that in a week or two he will feel as good as ever.

—Don Marquis

A husband and wife were at the hospital, awaiting the birth of their child. The doctor told them she had an experimental machine that could transfer some of the pain of childbirth from the mother to the father. The couple decided to give it a try. As the wife went into labor, the doctor set the machine at 10 percent, explaining that the man would probably feel more pain than he had ever known. To everyone's surprise, he felt no pain at all. The doctor slowly increased the percentage. The man still felt fine, and at last he asked to have all the pain. The amazed doctor honored his request, and the new mother concluded her delivery virtually pain-free. Afterward, the couple returned home with their new baby. As they pulled in the driveway, they saw their mailman—dead on the sidewalk.

"And most important," the doctor said, "be sure to drink plenty of fluids."

"Ah," the feverish patient replied, "there's my problem. I've been trying to drink solids!"

TV MEDICINE

Old Doctor: [upon delivering a baby] Ahh, it's a bouncing baby boy. Another ready soldier in the war against communism.

—Scrubs

One of the common birth defects suffered by babies who were subjected to crack cocaine in utero is the lack of one or both eyelids. The latest medical research has discovered that the foreskin from circumcised male babies can be surgically attached to replace the missing eyelids.

Results are generally positive, with the only long-term complication being that many of these post-surgery children became a little cockeyed!

A married couple was in a terrible accident in which the woman's face was severely burned. The doctor told the husband that they couldn't graft any skin from her body because she was too thin, so the husband offered to donate some of his own skin. The only skin on his body that the doctor felt was suitable would have to come from his backside. The husband and wife agreed that they would tell no one about where the skin came from and requested that the doctor also honor their secret.

The surgery was a complete success. Afterward, the woman was overcome with emotion at her husband's sacrifice. She said, "Dear, I just want to thank you for everything you did for me. There is no way I could ever repay you."

"My darling," he replied, "think nothing of it. I get all the reward I need every time I see your mother kiss you on the cheek."

For three days after death, hair and fingernails continue to grow but phone calls taper off.

—Johnny Carson

◆

Little-Known Illnesses

HYPOCOINDRIA
Fear of not having correct change.

SONSTROKE
An attack brought on by the reading of a will.

HERPES CINEPLEX
Rash caused by movie tickets priced at $9.50.

TV MEDICINE

Lisa: Hello, hospital? This is Lisa Simpson.
Hospital Operator: Simpson? Look, we've
already been down there tonight for a sisterectomy,
a case of severe butt rot, and a Leprechaun fight.
How dumb do you think we are?

—The Simpsons

We have not lost faith, but we have transferred it from God to the medical profession.

—George Bernard Shaw

◆

Things the Patient Shouldn't Hear During Surgery

• Could you stop that thing from beating? It's throwing my concentration off.
• I hate it when they're missing stuff in here.
• Don't worry. I think it's sharp enough.

STRANGE BUT TRUE MEDICAL FACTS

Statistical studies conducted in the 1990s point to a telling medical phenomenon: lowering blood cholesterol is good for the heart but appears to correlate to depression and deaths from suicide, violence, and accidents.

It should be the function of medicine to
help people die young as late in life as possible.

—Dr. Ernst Wunder, president of the
American Health Foundation

A young doctor had just opened her practice and was feeling nervous. When the nurse told her that a man was there to see her, she said to send him in. Wanting to look busy, she picked up the phone just as the man was coming in. "Yes, that's right. The fee is $200. Yes, I'll expect you at ten past two . . . All right. No later. My schedule is very tight." She hung up and turned to the man waiting. "May I help you?"

"Sorry, kid," the man said. "I'm just here to connect the phone."

Doctor: I have some bad news and some very bad news.
Patient: Might as well give me the bad news first.
Doctor: The lab called with your test results. They said you have twenty-four hours to live.
Patient: Twenty-four hours! That's terrible! What could be worse?
Doctor: I've been trying to reach you since yesterday.

TV MEDICINE

Dr. Kelso: Dr. Dorian, I owe you an apology; obviously I was unclear when I said, "Stay in the MRI room with that patient." It must have sounded like, "Leave and do other things."

—Scrubs

The room was full of pregnant women and their partners; the Lamaze class in full swing. In the course of her teaching, the instructor said, "Ladies, exercise is good for you. Walking is especially beneficial. And gentlemen, it wouldn't hurt you to go walking with your partner!" The room got quiet. Finally, one of the men raised his hand and asked, "Is it all right if she carries a golf bag while we walk?"

In recent years, more money has been spent on breast implants and Viagra than on Alzheimer's disease research, leading one to wonder: By the year 2030, will there be a large number of people wandering around with big breasts and erections who can't remember what to do with them?

Wherever the art of medicine is loved,
there also is a love of humanity.
—Hippocrates

Best Reported Allergies

- Nitrous oxide — "Makes me light-headed."
- Novocaine — "Makes me numb."
- Bleach — "When I inhale it, I have respiratory distress."
- Epinephrine — "Makes my heart race."

Just once I'd like to say to that doctor, "You know, I'm not ready for you yet. Why don't you go back in that little office and I'll be with you in a moment. And get your pants off."

—Jerry Seinfeld

Concluding his exam, the doctor said to his patient, "Mr. Franklin, I find very little wrong with you. You are in surprisingly good health despite being quite overweight. My advice to you is this: If you want to stay healthy, give up those intimate little dinners for two unless you have someone to share them with."

◆

How can you tell that managed care
has cut into your doctor's income?

He takes Friday off to play miniature golf.

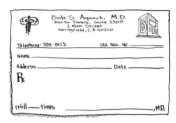

Things you don't want to hear from your doctor: "I'd tell you what your condition is, but I'm not sure how to pronounce it."

Medicine is a collection of uncertain prescriptions the results of which, taken collectively, are more fatal than useful to mankind.

—Napoleon Bonaparte

New Medications for Women

JackAsspirin—Relieves headache caused by a man who can't remember birthdays, anniversaries, or phone numbers.

Antitalksident—A spray carried in a purse or wallet to be used on anyone too eager to share their life stories with total strangers.

Sexcedrin—More effective than Excedrin in treating the "Not now, dear, I have a headache" syndrome.

An Irishman named O'Malley went to his doctor after a long illness.

The doctor said, "I've some bad news. You have cancer. I'd give you two weeks to live."

O'Malley was shocked, but he managed to compose himself, and as he left the office he told the news to his son, who had been waiting for him. O'Malley said, "Well son, we Irish celebrate when things are good, and we celebrate when things don't go so well. Let's head for the pub and have a few pints."

After three or four pints, their moods began to improve. They were eventually approached by some of O'Malley's old friends, who asked what the two were celebrating. O'Malley told them that the Irish celebrate the good and the bad. He told his friends, "I've only got a few weeks to live as I have been diagnosed with AIDS." The friends gave

O'Malley their condolences, and they had a couple more pints.

After the friends left, O'Malley's son leaned over and whispered his confusion. "Dad, I thought you said you were dying from cancer!"

O'Malley said, "I am dying of cancer, son. I just don't want any of them sleeping with your mother after I'm gone."

Or It's FREE!

Operating Room: Correct extremity amputated or it's FREE!

OB/GYN: It's your baby or it's FREE!

Pharmacy: It's the right medication or it's FREE!

Foley catheter insertions: Goes into the correct orifice or it's FREE!

Circumcision: Done right, or half off!

Before undergoing a surgical operation, arrange your temporal affairs. You may live.

—Ambrose Bierce

An elderly woman goes into the local newspaper office to place an obituary for her recently deceased husband. The editor informs her that the fee for the obituary is 50 cents a word. She pauses, reflects, and then says, "Well, then, let it read, 'Billy Bob died.'" Amused at the woman's thrift, the editor says, "Sorry, ma'am, there is a seven-word minimum on obituaries." Only a little flustered, she thinks things over and in a few seconds says, "In that case, let it read, 'Billy Bob died; 1983 pickup for sale.'"

Best Reported Allergies

- Novocaine — "When it wore off I had a lot of pain."

- Diprovan — "I lose consciousness."

- Paper tape — "Causes tachycardia."

- Poison ivy — "Gives me a rash."

A surgeon was checking on a patient who had a hernia operation three days before. The doctor asked the man why he hadn't yet gotten out of bed. "I hurt," the man replied. "You don't know how it feels." "I know exactly how it feels," the doctor said. "I had the same procedure last month, and I was back at work two days later. There's no difference in our operations." "Oh yes there is," said the patient. "You had a different surgeon."

A woman asks her husband if he'd like some breakfast. "Would you like bacon and eggs, perhaps? A slice of toast? Grapefruit and coffee to follow?"

He declines. "It's this Viagra," he says. "It's really taken the edge off my appetite."

At lunchtime, she asks if he would like something. "A bowl of soup, a cheese sandwich?" she inquires.

He declines. "It's this Viagra," he says. "It's really taken the edge off my appetite."

Come dinnertime, she asks if he wants anything to eat. "Would you like a steak? Maybe a pizza?"

He declines. "It's this Viagra," he says. "It's really taken the edge off my appetite."

"Well," she says, "would you mind letting me up, then? I'm starving!"

How does a doctor commit suicide?

He jumps down from his ego to his IQ.

STRANGE BUT TRUE MEDICAL FACTS

Fifteenth-century surgeon Guido Lanfranc used a musical method to detect skull fractures. He would have his patient clasp a violin string between the teeth, then he would pull the string taut and pluck it. If the resulting note came out clearly, the skull was fine; if the note was fuzzy, the skull was broken.

———◆———

A man went to a psychiatrist. "Doc," he said, "I've got trouble. Every time I get into bed, I think there's somebody under it. Then I get under the bed, and I think there's somebody on top of it. Doc, you've gotta help me!"

"Just put yourself in my hands for two years," said the psychiatrist. "Come to me three times a week, and I'll cure your fears."

"How much do you charge?"

"My fee is $140 per visit."

"That's a lot of dough," the man reckoned. "Let me think about it, and I'll get back to you."

Six months later, the doctor and the prospective patient crossed paths. "Why didn't you come to see me again?" asked the psychiatrist.

"At your prices? Heck, a bartender cured me for free!"

"And how exactly did he do that?"

"He told me to cut the legs off the bed!"

———◆———

Keeping off a large weight loss is a phenomenon about as common in American medicine as an impoverished dermatologist.

—Calvin Trillin

TRUE TALE

A long-term-care patient asked her nurse to stop giving her so much late sex because it kept her up all night. The nurse was puzzled as to what she could mean, until she tried to give the patient her Lasix dose. The patient replied that she got too much late sex and that's why she was up all night going to the bathroom.

A doctor was having an affair with his nurse. Before long, she told him she was pregnant. Not wanting his wife to know, he gave the nurse a sum of money and asked her to go to Italy and have the baby there.

"But how will I let you know that the baby is born?" she asked.

"Just send me a postcard and write 'spaghetti' on the back. I'll take care of expenses."

Not knowing what else to do, the nurse took the money and flew to Italy. Six months later the doctor's wife called him at the office and explained, "Dear, you received a very strange postcard in the mail today from Europe, and I don't understand what it means."

The doctor said, "Don't worry. I'll explain it when I get home."

Later that evening the doctor came home, read the postcard, and fell to the floor with a heart attack. Paramedics rushed him to the hospital. The lead medic stayed back to comfort the wife. He asked what trauma had precipitated the cardiac arrest. The wife picked up the postcard and read:

"Spaghetti, Spaghetti, Spaghetti. Two with sausage and meatballs, one without."

TV MEDICINE

Margaret "Hot Lips" Houlihan:
This isn't a hospital! It's an insane asylum!
And it's your fault!

—M*A*S*H

One of the most difficult things to contend
with in a hospital is the assumption on the part
of the staff that because you have lost your
gallbladder you have also lost your mind.

—Jean Kerr

———◆◆◆———

The most extreme case of specialization on record is the Washington, D.C., doctor who treats only U.S. senators. He refuses to make House calls.

◆

You've Been an ER Doctor Too Long If . . .

• you mistake the new resident for a high school volunteer.

• you either know the diagnosis in the first thirty seconds or you send the patient home without one.

• you want to post a sign saying, "If you're on Fen-Phen, go home. There's nothing wrong."

• the baby you delivered your first year of practice just came in with a heroin overdose.

———◆◆◆———

The lawyer was deposing the doctor for a malpractice case . . .

Q: Doctor, before you performed the autopsy, did you check for a pulse?

A: No.

Q: Did you check for breathing or blood pressure?

A: No.

Q: So, then it's possible that the patient was alive when you began the autopsy?

A: No. His brain was sitting on my desk in a jar at the time.

Q: But could the patient have been alive nevertheless?

A: No . . . well, I suppose it's possible, if he was an attorney.

Little-Known Illnesses

AFROPHOBIA
Fear of the return of 1970s hairstyles.

PSEUDONYMPHOMANIA
The compulsive desire to have sex under
an assumed name.

DÉJA FLU
The feeling that you've had this cold before.

New Medications for Men

Flatulagra — This complex drug converts men's noxious intestinal gases back into food solids. Special bonus: Dosage can be doubled for long car rides.

Capagra — Caused test subjects to become uncharacteristically fastidious about lowering toilet seats and replacing toothpaste caps. Subjects on higher doses were seen dusting furniture.

Flyagra — This drug has been showing great promise in treating men with OFD (Open Fly Disorder). Especially useful for men on Viagra.

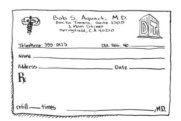

Strange but True Medical Facts

Egyptian doctors anticipated the advent of penicillin. Long before its discovery, they treated wounds by applying moldy bread.

Benefits of Becoming Senile

- You're always meeting new people.

- You never have to watch reruns on television.

- Mystery novels are always suspenseful.

- You can hide your own Easter eggs.

Preferred Games of Hospital Personnel

GASTROENTEROLOGISTS: Chutes and Ladders

ORTHOPEDISTS: Pinball

GENE THERAPISTS: Barrel of Monkeys

I was taken to the hospital for observation. I stayed several days, didn't observe anything, and left.

—George Carlin

———◆———

An ounce of prevention is worth a pound
of bandages and adhesive tape.

—Groucho Marx

```
Patient: Jane Doe                    Date: October 22, 2003   Time: 15:23
X-Ray of Pelvis area and lower back                Doctor I.M. Aquack
```

Three Good Reasons to Become a Doctor

- Free latex gloves

- Stylish scrubs

- The world doesn't need any more lawyers.

———◆———

The divorce attorney and the gynecologist were discussing the merits of their professions. Said the attorney, "I love my work. Every day women come into my office, tell me all their problems, and pay me good money for my advice."

The gynecologist topped him, though. "Well, in my line of work," he said, "women come into my office, take off their clothes, tell me their problems, and pay me good money for my advice."

Nothing is more fatal to health than overcare of it.

—Benjamin Franklin

What should men do if lost in the wilderness
with only their supply of daily medications?

Take Viagra and an iron supplement.
It will turn them into the perfect compass.

A seventy-five-year-old woman went to the doctor for a check-up. The doctor told her she needed more activity and recommended sex three times a week. She said to the doctor, "Please, tell my husband."

The doctor went out to the waiting room and told the husband that his wife needed to have sex three times a week. The eighty-year-old husband replied, "Which days?"

"How about Monday, Wednesday, and Friday?"

"I can bring her Mondays and Wednesdays," the man said, "but on Fridays she'll have to take the bus."

LITTLE-KNOWN ILLNESSES

CELESTIAL SEASONINGS AFFECTIVE DISORDER
Herbal-tea addiction.

VISACARDITIS
The sensation brought on by exceeding your credit limit.

ALPOPLEXY
Canine feeding disorder.

What do you give a man who has everything?

Penicillin.

STRANGE BUT TRUE MEDICAL FACTS

According to *The Guinness Book of World Records,* the world's largest gallbladder weighed twenty-three pounds. It was removed from a woman in Maryland in 1989.

I firmly believe that if the whole materia medica could be sunk to the bottom of the sea, it would be all the better for mankind, and all the worse for the fishes.

—Dr. Oliver Wendell Holmes

New Medications for Women

Buyagra—Injectable stimulant taken prior to shopping. Increases potency and duration of spending spree.

Extra Strength Buy-One-All—When combined with **Buyagra**, can cause an indiscriminate buying frenzy so severe the victim may even come home with a Donny Osmond CD or a book by Dr. Laura.

PREFERRED GAMES OF HOSPITAL PERSONNEL

Geriatric nurses: Bingo

Eating disorders specialists: Hungry Hungry Hippo

Financial officers: Trouble

◆

LITTLE-KNOWN ILLNESSES

STREISAND-BROLIN SYNDROME
The need to display excessive affection.

ROSWELL-BABY SYNDROME
The fear that one's infant might be an alien.

OREOPOROSIS
A disorder caused by too many cookies and not enough milk.

New Medications For Men

Directra—A dose of this drug given to men before leaving on car trips caused 72 percent of them to stop and ask for directions when they got lost, compared to a control group where only 2 percent asked for directions.

Projectra—Men given this experimental new drug were far more likely to actually finish a household repair project before starting a new one.

IT'S A FACT

A study, published in the *Journal of the American Medical Association*, demonstrated that increasing by one the number of patients in the average nurse's caseload had serious results: a 7 percent increase in the likelihood of surgical patients' death within thirty days of admission, not to mention a 15 percent increase in nurses' job dissatisfaction and a 23 percent increase in their rate of burnout.

If medicine is necessarily a mystery to the average man, nearly everything else is necessarily a mystery to the average doctor.

—Milton Mayer

Best Reported Allergies

• "Allergic to all painkillers except Demerol."

• "Allergic to all painkillers except one, called 'perc-asomething' but I really don't remember the exact name."

• "Allergic to Demerol, codeine, morphine, and 2mg Dilaudid. But I can take 4mg Dilaudid."

A ninety-year-old man went in for his annual checkup. When the doctor asked how he was feeling, he said, "Never been better! I've got an eighteen-year-old bride who's pregnant with my child! What do you think about that?"

The doctor considered this for a moment. "Let me tell you a story," he said. "I knew a guy who was an avid hunter. One day he went out in a hurry and accidentally grabbed his umbrella instead of his gun. He was in the woods and suddenly a grizzly bear appeared in front of him! He raised up his umbrella, pointed it at the bear, and squeezed the handle. And do you know what happened?"

"No," the old man said. "Tell me."

"The bear dropped dead in front of him!"

"That's impossible! Someone else must have shot that bear."

"That's kind of what I'm driving at," the doctor replied.

IT'S A FACT

Number of physicians in the United States: 700,000.

Accidental deaths caused by physicians per year: 120,000.

Accidental deaths per physician: 0.171 (U.S. Department of Health & Human Services)

Number of gun owners in the United States: 80,000,000.

Number of accidental gun deaths per year: 1,500.

Accidental deaths per gun owner per year: 0.0000188

Statistically, doctors are approximately 9,000 times more dangerous than gun owners.

A young man goes into a drugstore to buy condoms. The pharmacist says the condoms come in packs of three, nine, or twelve and asks which the young man wants. "Well," he says, "I've been seeing this girl for a while and she's really hot. I want the condoms because I think tonight's 'the' night. We're having dinner with her parents, and after that we're going out, and it's then I've got a feeling I'm gonna get lucky. Once we've done it, she'll want me all the time, so you'd better give me the twelve-pack."

Later that evening, the young man sits down to dinner with his girlfriend and her parents. He asks if he might give the blessing, and they agree. He begins the prayer, and continues praying for several minutes. The girl leans over and says, "You never told me that you were such a religious person." He leans over to her and whispers, "You never told me that your father is a pharmacist."

STRANGE BUT TRUE MEDICAL FACTS

Before the discovery of germs, it was commonly believed that disease was caused by miasma, an ill-smelling gas such as emanated from sewers and rotting flesh.

Giving birth is like pushing a piano through a transom.

—Alice Roosevelt Longworth

An elderly woman telephoned her son and said, "I called the doctor's office this morning, and when I spoke to the doctor she was so rude to me, I just couldn't believe it." The bewildered son phoned the doctor and demanded an explanation.

"I sincerely apologize," the doctor said. "Have you ever just had one of those days? At the moment your mother called there were two patients screaming at me, an insurance company was on the other line, and one of the nurses had just dropped a urine sample on my shoe. When your mother asked how to use a rectal thermometer, I just blurted out the first thing that came into my head."

But in both [hospitals and private houses],
let whoever is in charge keep this simple question
in her head (not, how can I always do this
right thing myself, but) how can I provide for
this right thing to be always done?

—Florence Nightingale

◆

NEW MEDICATIONS FOR MEN

Childagra—Men taking this drug reported a sudden, overwhelming urge to perform more child-care tasks—especially cleaning up spills and little accidents.

Complimentra—In clinical trials, 82 percent of middle-aged men administered this drug noticed that their wives had a new hairstyle. Currently being tested to see if its effects extend to noticing new clothing.

Not long ago, a teaching hospital installed a computer to interview patients visiting its gynecology department. Apparently the programmers were none too familiar with the nature of women's health. One of the questions the computer asked was, "Are you having your monthly period now?" If the answer was "yes," the computer would send the woman away and reschedule the appointment—for four weeks later.

SIGNS YOU'RE IN A BAD HOSPITAL

• In the operating room, you see a surgeon holding a sign that says, WILL DO SURGERY FOR FOOD!

• All the diplomas on the wall are signed by Sally Struthers.

• You and your roommate have to take turns on the IV.

• Through a fog of anesthesia, you hear a surgeon shouting, "Bring the damn Scotch tape! And plenty of it!"

• Instead of "patient," they use the term "plaintiff."

Doctors are just the same as lawyers; the only difference is that lawyers merely rob you whereas doctors rob you and kill you too.

—Anton Checkov

◆

Best Reported Allergies

- "I can only take brand-name drugs, I get a rash from any generics."

- "Allergic to oxygen."

- "Allergic to water."

- "Allergic to nonnarcotic pain relievers."

Why I Would Rather Work in Sick Bay
on the Enterprise

- Regardless of species, the patients never have to be undressed or helped out of bed.

- The patients never need any IV lines, monitor cables, or tubes.

- The patient never needs to be fed or bathed.

- The patient never vomits or defecates.

- The patient will be cured at the end of forty-six minutes unless he or she expires in the first five minutes.

SIGNS YOU NEED A NEW DOCTOR

• He refers to your legs as "drumsticks."

• He rents his examination room by the hour from the No-Tell Motel.

• His anesthesiologist is "Doctor Jack Daniels."

• After surgery, he asks if you'll be wanting a "to go" bag.

◆

Why would a doctor prescribe pain pills? I already have pain! I need relief pills!

—George Carlin

Three doctors and three nurses were traveling by train to a conference. At the station, the doctors bought tickets, while the nurses boarded with only a single ticket between them. The doctors watched as the nurses crammed into a restroom. When the conductor came around collecting tickets, he knocked on the restroom door and a single arm emerged with a ticket in hand. The conductor took it and moved on.

The doctors agreed this was a clever idea and decided to do the same on the return trip. At the station, they were astonished to see that the nurses didn't buy a ticket at all. Upon boarding, the doctors crammed into a restroom, and the nurses did the same in another one nearby.

The train departed, and shortly afterward one of the nurses left his restroom, walked over to the restroom where the doctors were hiding, and knocked on the door. "Ticket, please," he said.

MEMO
To: All Doctors
Subject: Sick Leave Policy

Doctors' notes will no longer be accepted as proof of illness. If you are well enough to go to a doctor's office, you are well enough to come to work.

THE RULES OF EMTS

- Sick people don't complain.
- Air goes in and out, blood goes round and round. Any variation on this is a bad thing.
- The more equipment you see on an EMT's belt, the newer he is.
- When dealing with patients, supervisors, or citizens, if it felt good saying it, it was the wrong thing to say.

Always laugh when you can. It is cheap medicine.

—Lord Byron

"Mrs. Smith," said the nurse to a seriously ill patient, "I'm afraid I've got some really bad news for you. The doctor has informed me that you've tested positive for VD, AIDS, and ebola virus."

"Oh, no! What treatment can you give me?"

"We're going to take you into the hospital, give you your own private room, and put you on a diet of veal cutlets and pancakes."

"Veal cutlets and pancakes? Delicious! I never realized that those delicious foods could help cure me!"

"They won't, but they're easy to slide under the door."

Intern Pop Quiz

You are assisting a fellow intern with charcoal administration down an orogastric tube. The room measures eight feet by twelve feet. The patient starts to vomit before the tube is pulled. Knowing that charcoal can spew out of a tube in a five-foot radius (even with a thumb over the opening) and the stretcher is only two feet wide, how many feet per second do you have to back up to get less charcoal on you than on your fellow intern?

An American businessman traveled throughout the Pacific Rim on a three-month business trip. He mixed business with pleasure once too often and contracted a mysterious venereal disease. His home physician informed him that his member would have to be amputated. Shocked that his doctor would propose such a radical procedure, the businessman consulted numerous other physicians, but they all said the same thing.

Suddenly, it occurred to him that if he contracted this disease in the Far East, he should consult an Eastern doctor, one who specializes in traditional Asian medicine. So he asked around, and made an appointment with a traditional healer in New York's Chinatown. The businessman explained his problems and what his doctors had told him, and asked if amputation were really the only cure.

"No, I don't think amputation is necessary at all," said the Asian doctor. The patient was tremendously relieved.

"That's great! I saw dozens of doctors and they all said amputation was the only way."

"Bah!! What do Western doctors know?" scoffed the Chinese healer with disdain.

"Any doctor worth his salt could tell you that it'll drop off by itself in four to six weeks!"

A cheerful heart is good medicine, but a crushed spirit dries up the bones.

—Proverbs 17:22

◆

BEST REPORTED ALLERGIES

- Cortisone —"Gives me hives."
- Morphine —"Makes me sleepy."
- Ampicillin — "Gives me a yeast infection."
- Cortisone/prednisone — "Makes me puffy."

RADIO MEDICINE

Transfusion, transfusion
My body's just a mass of contusions
I'll never speed again—
Slip a gallon to me, Alan.

— *"Transfusion"*
1950s novelty song by Nervous Norvus

TV MEDICINE

Julie: This drug is the best one on the market. The only side effects are nausea, impotence, and anal leakage.

Dr. Cox: And I'm getting two out of three, just from having this conversation!

—Scrubs

Do Roman paramedics refer to IVs as "4's?"

—Stephen Wright

SIGNS YOU'RE IN A BAD HOSPITAL

• You go in for routine surgery, you come out with a tail.

• You recognize your doctor as the kid who was mopping the lobby when you checked in.

• Instead of a sponge bath, they send a Saint Bernard to lick you.

• As you're going under, your surgeon says, "Man, am I baked!"

• Every couple of minutes, you hear a bugle playing *"Taps."*

An alternative to blood transfusion was tried in Toronto in 1854 during a cholera epidemic: transfusion of cow's milk. The underlying rationale was that milk would turn into white blood cells. Of the seven patients treated by intravenous transfusion of twelve ounces of milk, five died but two allegedly got better.

—R.F. Mould, *Mould's Medical Anecdotes*

◆

No illness which can be treated by the diet should be treated by any other means.

—Moses Malmonides of Caldova

Two doctors opened an office in a small town and put up a sign reading, "Dr. Wilkins and Dr. Erving, Psychiatry and Proctology." The town council was not pleased with the sign, so the doctors altered it to read, "Minds and Behinds." This was not acceptable either, so they tried again with, "Schizoids and Hemorrhoids." Another thumbs down. Next they proposed, "Catatonics and High Colonics." Still no go. Then came, "Manic-depressives and Anal-retentives." No again. "Hysterias and Posteriors." Unacceptable . . . as were "Analysis and Anal Cysts," "Nuts and Butts," "Freaks and Cheeks," and "Loons and Moons." Near wits' end, the doctors made one final proposal, which to their eternal relief the council accepted: "Dr. Wilkins and Dr. Erving, Odds and Ends."

THE RULES OF EMTS

• All bleeding stops . . . eventually.

• If the patient vomits in the rig, try to make sure it's on the disposable equipment, not the stuff you have to clean.

• There will be problems.

• You can't cure stupid.

◆

Statistics say that accidental deaths in hospitals are four times more likely to happen than death in an auto accident. You know what this means if you get in a car accident: don't go to the hospital!

—Jay Leno

A woman went to her OB-GYN for her first checkup after learning she was pregnant. The doctor gave her a clean bill of health, and then stamped her stomach with a tiny line of indelible ink.

The woman returned home and, curious to find out what the doctor was up to, dug out her magnifying glass. She could make out in tiny letters across her belly: "When you can read this, come back and see me."

One of my problems is that I internalize everything.
I can't express anger—I grow a tumor instead.

—Woody Allen

◆

You've Been an ER Doctor Too Long If . . .

- you think modesty and religion are just impediments to good medical care.

- you know the sign language for "shot," "pain," and "X-ray."

- you assume new ER nurses should know what you want, and should do it without being told.

- you no longer leave the room when the portable X-rays are taken.

The HMO account manager noticed that nearly every bill from one pediatrician's office included the line item "behavior modification reinforcers."

Fearing that the pediatrician was engaging in some unapproved, experimental psychological treatment, she called the pediatrician's office to inquire, "What on earth are behavior modification reinforcers?"

"Lollipops," was the reply.

THE RULES OF EMTS

- If it's wet and sticky and not yours, leave it alone.

- The severity of the injury is directly proportional to the difficulty in accessing the patient, multiplied by the patient's weight.

- There is no such thing as a "textbook case."

- If there are no drunks at an MVA after midnight, keep looking—someone is missing.

Why did the guru refuse novocaine
when he went to his dentist?

He wanted to transcend dental medication.

You hear about the latest wonder drug?

When administered to women, it gives them the irresistible urge to join a convent. The FDA refuses to approve it, though. They fear it will be habit-forming.

◆

Preferred Games of Hospital Personnel

Administrators: Trivial Pursuit

Plastic surgeons: Mr. Potato Head

Podiatrists: Tic Tac Toe

A doctor in a bar leans over to the guy on the next stool and says, "Wanna hear a managed care joke?"

"Well, before you tell that joke," the neighbor replies, "you should know something. I'm six feet tall, 200 pounds, and I'm a managed care lawyer. The guy sitting next to me is six-two, 225 pounds, and he's a managed care executive. The fellow next to him is six-foot-five, weighs 250 if he weighs a pound, and he's one of our second-level reviewers. Now, you still wanna tell that joke?"

"Nah," the doctor says. "I don't want to have to explain it three times."

◆

A hospital should also have a recovery room adjoining the cashier's office.

—Francis O'Walsh

A man was walking down the street when he came across a body lying on the sidewalk. He ran to a phone and called 911.

The operator asked him where he was, and the man replied, "I'm on Sycamore Boulevard."

"How do you spell that?" the operator asked.

"S-i-c-k . . ." the man began. "No, s-i-c-a . . . no, s-i-k-a . . . oh heck, let me drag him over to Elm Street and I'll call you back."

Bob S. Aquack, M.D.
Doctor Towers, Suite 1305
1 Main Street
Springfield, CA 90210

Telephone: 555-0123   DEA. REG. NO. _____

NAME _____

Address _____ Date _____

R_x

refill ___ times _____ , M.D.

A ninety-two-year-old man went to the doctor to get a physical. A few days later the doctor saw the man walking down the street with a gorgeous young lady on his arm.

At his follow-up visit the doctor talked to the man and said, "You're really doing great, aren't you?"

The man replied, "Just following doctor's orders. You said, 'Get a hot mama and be cheerful'."

The doctor chuckled, "I didn't say that at all. I said you've got a heart murmur. Be careful."

A neurotic is the person who builds a castle in the air. A psychotic is the person who lives in it. And a psychiatrist is the person who collects the rent.

◆

When I had my operation, the doctor gave me a local anesthetic. I couldn't afford the imported kind.

—Laugh-In

After hearing that one of the patients in a mental hospital had saved another from a suicide attempt by pulling him out of a bathtub, the director reviewed the rescuer's file and called him into his office.

"Mr. Smith," the director said, "your history here and your heroic behavior indicate that you're ready to go home. I'm only sorry that the man you saved later killed himself by hanging."

"Oh, he didn't kill himself," the patient replied. "I hung him up to dry."

POSTED ON THE LAB DOOR:

SUPPORT BACTERIA.
They're the only culture some people have.

The patient is dying, slowly and horribly. Yet nobody can figure out what's wrong. He's been in the hospital for a week. Now his blood pressure is slipping, his bone marrow has failed, and his kidneys have shut down. The doctors decide to stop treatment and leave him alone with his wife as he dies.

"Honey, there's something I have to tell you," the patient whispers. "I've been unfaithful to you. I've been sleeping with my secretary for the last three years."

His wife leans close. "I've known about it for some time. It's okay now."

"And the diamond in your ring? I had it replaced with a cubic zirconia and spent the money on golf clubs." The words come in gasps, as the patient clings to his few remaining minutes of life.

"A friend at the jewelry store told me. It's okay now."

The patient turns a shade more blue. "And when I was on that so-called business trip last month? I was in Las Vegas, where I gambled away our children's college fund!"

"I knew about it. But everything's okay now." his wife whispers.

"Oh, you're a saint!" the man gasps. "How can you say it's okay, after what I've done?"

The wife glances at the door, then leans closer. "Because, dear, I'm the one who poisoned you."

WHAT AMBULANCE DRIVERS DO FOR FUN

- Drive too fast over speed bumps
- Run the siren while filling up at the gas station
- Stop to ask for directions
- Watch the movie *Mother, Jugs, and Speed . . .* over and over again

What form of contraception does an anesthetist use?

His personality.

Reading Habits of the Medical Profession

Medical student: Reads entire article in medical journal but does not understand what any of it means.

Intern: Skips the article but reads the classifieds.

Resident: Uses journal as a pillow during nights on call.

Practicing doctor: Doesn't read journals, but keeps an eye open for medical articles in *Time* or *Newsweek*.

Dean of medical school: Reads entire article in medical journal but does not understand what any of it means.

PREFERRED GAMES OF HOSPITAL PERSONNEL

Cardiologists: *Hearts*
Cafeteria workers: *Mousetrap*
Proctologists: *Poker*

Three expectant fathers sat in a Minneapolis hospital waiting room while their wives were in labor. The nurse arrived and announced to the first man, "Congratulations, you're the father of twins."

"What a coincidence," he said. "I work for the Minnesota Twins."

The nurse returned in a little while and told the second man, "You, sir, are the father of triplets."

"Wow, what an incredible coincidence," he exclaimed. "I work for 3M Corporation."

The first two men were passing out cigars when they noticed the third man sitting in the corner, white as a sheet.

"Hey, buddy, don't worry," said the first

man. "I'm sure your wife will deliver soon."

The third man didn't reply; he only muttered to himself, "Why did I take that job at 7-Eleven? Why did I take that job at 7-Eleven? . . ."

How many surgeons does it take to change a light bulb?

None. They'd wait for a suitable donor and do a filament transplant.

TV MEDICINE

Titus: *My dad's third heart attack, he'd gotten so good at them, he decided to drive himself to the hospital because "They won't let me smoke in the ambulance!" and "You can't make a burger run."*

—Titus

It's like a convent, the hospital. You leave the world behind and take vows of poverty, chastity, obedience.

—Carolyn Wheat

An optometrist was instructing a new employee on how to charge a customer. "As you are fitting his glasses, if he asks how much they cost, you say '$150.'

"If his eyes don't flutter, say, 'For the frames. The lenses will be $100.'

"If his eyes still don't flutter, you add, 'Each.'"

A doctor got a phone call from one of his colleagues. "We need a fourth for poker," the voice on the phone said.

"I'll be right over," replied the doctor.

As he was putting on his overcoat, his wife asked, "Is it serious?"

"Oh yes, quite serious," he said gravely. "They've had to call in three other doctors as well."

One of the Great Things About Being a Doctor

When your non-medical friends are complaining about their workday you can say, "Did anybody die? Well, then it wasn't so bad, was it?"

TV MEDICINE

Dr. Carter: If you don't know what it's called, you sure as hell shouldn't be using it.

—E.R.

*A trip to the hospital is always a descent
into the macabre. I have never
trusted a place with shiny floors.*

—Terry Tempest Williams

Preferred Games of Hospital Personnel

Surgeons: *Operation*

Clinic personnel: *Ants in the Pants*

Urologists: *Upwords*

Who ever thought up the word "mammogram?"
Every time I hear it, I think I'm supposed to put my
breast in an envelope and send it to someone.

—Jan King

IT'S A FACT

More than 3 in 10 of the 3 billion prescriptions filled each
year in the United States have to be rechecked with the
doctor, most notably because of confusion over the doctor's handwriting.

I recently had a ringing in my ear. The doctors looked inside and found a small bell.

—George Carlin

A man called his doctor and said, "Doctor, it appears that my wife has come down with a case of laryngitis."

"Bring her into the office, then," the doctor said, "and I'll see what I can do to treat the condition."

"Actually, I was hoping you could tell me how to prolong it."

An orthopedic surgeon was moving to a new office, with the help of his staff. One of the nurses sat the display skeleton in the front of her car, a bony arm across the back of the seat.

On the drive across town, she stopped at a traffic light, and the stares of the people in the neighboring car compelled her to roll down her window and yell, "I'm delivering him to my doctor's office."

The other driver leaned out of his window. "I hate to tell you, lady," he said, "but I think it's too late!"

Overheard During a Prostate Exam
"You used to be an executive at Enron, didn't you?"

◆

A man with a worried look on his face ran into the ER and asked the first doctor he saw if she knew a way to stop the hiccups. Without any warning, the doctor slapped him in the face. Amazed and angry, the young man demanded an explanation for this unusual behavior.

"Well," said the doctor, "you don't have the hiccups now, do you?"

"No," the young man answered, "but my wife out in the car still does."

When a physician remarked on a new patient's extraordinarily ruddy complexion, he said, "High blood pressure, Doc. It runs in my family."

"Your mother's side or your father's?" the physician asked.

"Neither," the patient replied. "It's from my wife's family."

"Oh, come now," said the physician. "How could your wife's family give you high blood pressure?"

He sighed. "You oughta meet 'em sometime, Doc!"

◆

In hospitals there is no time off for good behavior.

—Josephine Tey

A tightfisted businessman broke his hip. He hired the most esteemed surgeon in town to put him back together, which required lining up the broken hip and putting in a screw to secure it. The operation was successful, and the surgeon charged the businessman a fee of $5,000 for his services. The businessman was outraged by the amount charged and sent the surgeon a letter demanding an itemized bill. The doctor complied, sending back the following list:

> One screw: $1
>
> Knowing how to put it in: $4,999
>
> Total: $5,000

Passing through the hospital corridors, a doctor noticed a strong smell of marijuana. He asked one of the nurses on duty about the odor. "The good thing," the nurse said, "is that down that hall everybody's glaucoma has cleared up. The bad thing is that now everyone wants a Twinkie!"

Hospitals are only an intermediate stage of civilization.

—Florence Nightingale

A doctor was preparing to examine an elderly lady. He noticed that she was a little nervous, so he began to tell her a story as he put on his surgical gloves. "Do you know how they make these gloves?" he asked.

"No," she replied, "How?"

"Well, in the glove factory there's a large tank of latex. The workers, who are lined up according to hand size, walk up to the tank, dip their hands in, and then walk around until the latex dries right onto their hands! Then they peel off the gloves and start the process all over again."

Seeing that he wasn't getting the laugh he had hoped for, the doctor began the exam without further delay. Five minutes later, the woman began to giggle.

"I'm sorry," she said, blushing. "It just occurred to me how they must make condoms!"

TV MEDICINE

Patient: *I'll sue his ass!*
Dr. Green: *That's very American of you.*

—E.R.

A sixteen-year-old patient signed himself in at the office of Dr. James Holder of Brooklyn. On a form required for new patients, the young man looked at the list of medical complaints and checked off "Penile Drainage" and "Burning with Urination." Under "Responsible Party," he listed his girlfriend's name.

—Allan Zullo (with Martha Moffett), *Sick Humor: Outrageous but True Medical Stories from the ER to the OR*

A doctor was performing a checkup on an esteemed army general. At one point during the exam the doctor said, "If you don't mind my asking, sir, when was the last time you had sex?"

"Of course, I understand, medical reasons and all that," the general answered. "I would say approximately 1975."

"So, you've been inactive for quite some time."

"You think so?" The general checked his watch. "It's only 2140 now."

Medical Chart Bloopers

"Pt complaining of headache. Tylenol given as ordered. Checked back with pt one hour later and head gone."

*Looking out of a hospital window is
different from looking out of any other.
Somehow you do not see outside.*
—Carol Matthau

A man with multiple bruises and lacerations rushed to his doctor's office one day. "Doctor, I just don't understand," the man said. "I think I'm a bridge." "My goodness," the doctor said. "What's come over you?"

"One semi, a pickup truck, and two cars."

It's a Fact
*Fifty percent of all doctors graduate at
the bottom half of their class.*

STRANGE BUT TRUE MEDICAL STORIES

A surgical resident was called out of a sound sleep to the emergency room. Unshaven and with tousled hair, he showed up with an equally unpresentable medical student.

In the ER they encountered the on-call medical resident and his student, both neatly attired in clean white lab coats. The resident said to his student, "You can always tell the surgeons by their absolute disregard for appearance."

Two evenings later, the surgical resident was at a banquet when called to the ER to suture a minor laceration. He was stitching away—still wearing a tuxedo from the event—when he encountered that same medical resident, who looked at him, then said to his student, "Sure is sensitive to criticism, isn't he?"

New Medications for Women

Damitol—Take two and the rest of the world can go to hell for up to eight hours.

St. Mom's Wort—Plant extract that treats mom's depression by rendering preschoolers unconscious for up to six hours.

Empty Nestrogen—Highly effective suppository that eliminates melancholy by enhancing the memory of how awful your kids were as teenagers, and how you couldn't wait until they moved out.

◆

You can learn a lot about paranoids just
by following them around.

A doctor was walking into the hospital when she saw a man doubled over in pain in the parking lot. "Can I help you?" she asked. "Are you here to see one of the doctors?"

"Well, I was," the man said, "but I got to the office door and it said on it 'Dr. Bortnick, 9 to 1.' With those odds, I figured I was better off taking care of myself."

◆

A survey taken a few years ago asked 10,000 U.S. nurses if they'd willingly choose to be patients in their own hospitals. Thirty-eight percent said "No way."

—*Doctors Killed George Washington*,
by Erin Barrett and Jack Mingo

The ultimate indignity is to be given a bedpan by a stranger who calls you by your first name.

—Maggie Kuhn

Preferred Games of Hospital Personnel

Doctors of infectious disease: *Risk*

Psychiatrists: *Outburst*

Neurologists: *Concentration*

A pediatric patient who was vomiting and running a high fever was given an aspirin suppository. When the doctor later asked the patient how he was feeling, he replied that he would rather have had a "mouthprin."

◆

What Ambulance Drivers Do for Fun

- Replace the siren with the music of an ice-cream van.
- Put a disco ball in the rear of the ambulance.
- Toss cuts of raw meat out the back door.
- Drive around the graveyard.

MEMO
To: Medical Personnel
From: Human Resources

It has come to our attention from several emergency rooms that many EMT narratives have taken a decidedly creative direction lately. Effective immediately, all members are to refrain from using slang and abbreviations to describe patients, such as the following:

• Descriptions of a car crash do not have to include phrases like "negative vehicle to vehicle interface" or "terminal deceleration syndrome."

• Endotracheal intubation is not to be referred to as a "PVC Challenge."

• Do not refer to recently deceased persons as being "paws up," ART (assuming room temperature), CC (Cancel Christmas), CTD (circling the drain), or NLPR (no long playing records).

The patient told the doctor he hadn't been feeling well. She considered his symptoms, looked him over, and then gave him three bottles of pills. "Take the green pill with a big glass of water when you wake up," she told him. "Take the blue pill with a big glass of water after you eat lunch. Then just before going to bed, take the red pill with another big glass of water."

"That's some regimen," the patient said. "What exactly is wrong with me?"

"You're not drinking enough water."

You Might Be an ER Doctor If . . .

• The hospital's attorney wants to talk to you, but her secretary won't tell you what it's about.

• In the middle of a disaster drill, two real trauma patients present themselves.

◆

Hospitals, like airports and supermarkets,
only pretend to be open nights and weekends.

—Molly Haskell

◆

TV MEDICINE

Dr. Morganstern: Give me a good sick body, needs a little slicing, and I'm a happy man.

—E.R.

In the hills of Tennessee, a farmer's wife went into labor in the middle of the night, and the doctor was called out to assist in the delivery. There was no electricity, so the doctor handed the father-to-be a lantern and said, "Here, hold this high so I can see what I'm doing." Soon, a baby boy was brought into the world.

"Don't be in a rush to put the lantern down," said the doctor. "I think there's another one to come." Sure enough, within minutes she had delivered a baby girl.

"Keep holding that lantern," she said. "It seems there's yet another one in there!"

The farmer scratched his head in bewilderment and asked, "Do you think it's the light that's attractin' 'em?"

A_t the beginning of the school year, the dean came into the lecture hall and said a general, "Good morning" to everyone there. When the students returned his greeting, he said, "Ah, you're freshmen." He explained how he could tell.

"When you walk in and say good morning, and they say good morning back, they're freshmen. When they put their newspapers down and open their books, they're sophomores. When they look up so they can see the instructor over the tops of the newspapers, they're juniors. When they put their feet up on the desks and keep reading, they're seniors."

"When you walk in and say good morning, and they write it down, they're medical students."

An American surgeon lecturing medical students in Bristol, England, was asked if he considered the operation he was describing a valuable one. "Valuable?" demanded the surgeon, a little taken aback. "I raised five kids on it."

—Financial Times

What's the difference between a psychiatrist and a magician?

A psychiatrist pulls habits out of rats.

Hospital rooms seem to have vastly more ceiling than any rooms people live in.

—Bertha Damon

◆

People love to recommend their doctor to you. I don't know what they get out of it, but they really push them on you. "Is he good?" "He's the best. This guy's the best." There can't be this many "bests." Someone's graduating at the bottom of these classes. Where are these doctors? Is someone somewhere saying to their friend, "You should see my doctor, he's the worst. He's the absolute worst there is. Whatever you've got, it'll be worse after you see him. The man's an absolute butcher."

—Jerry Seinfeld

How to Distinguish Medical School from Hell

• You won't have to take out a loan to go to hell.

• You might have a chance to get some sleep in hell.

• Hell lasts for eternity. (Medical school just feels that way.)

TV MEDICINE

"So, Mr. Clinton, tell me, what do you think of this new wonder drug, Viagra?"

"It's like they found a way to put twenty-three-year-old interns in a bottle."

—Conan O'Brien

New Medications for Women

Antiboyotics—When administered to teenage girls, is highly effective in improving grades, freeing up phone lines, and reducing money spent on makeup.

Menicillin—Potent antiboyotic for older women. Increases resistance to such lines as, "You make me want to be a better person . . . can we get naked now?"

◆

A sweet young lady visited her gynecologist. "Doctor," she asked, "my boyfriend wants to try oral sex. Can I get pregnant from oral sex?"

"Heavens, yes, girl. Where do you think HMO executives come from?"

An elderly gentleman went to see his doctor and asked for a prescription of Viagra. The doctor said, "That's no problem. How many do you want?"

The man answered, "Just a few, maybe four, but cut each one into quarters."

The doctor said, "That won't do you any good."

The elderly gentleman said, "That's all right. I'm ninety years old, I don't need them for sex anymore. I just don't want to pee on my shoes.

There's a lot of people in this world who
spend so much time watching their health
that they haven't the time to enjoy it.

—Josh Billings

Things Not to Do While You Are with Your Wife in Labor in the Delivery Room

• Clip your toenails.

• Read *Playboy*.

• Tell the doctor that you want the afterbirth to have it bronzed.

• Flirt with the nurse.

• Watch a football game on your portable television.

• Tell her how pretty and sexy she looks right now.

Whenever a friend refers a doctor they say, "Make sure that you tell him that you know me." Why? What's the difference? He's a doctor. "Oh, you know Bob? Oh, okay, I'll give you the real medicine. Everybody else I'm giving Tic-Tacs."

—Jerry Seinfeld

DR. ROSS: Fine couple of doctors we are, huh?

DR. GREEN: Remember when we were going to change the world?

DR. ROSS: No. I was always in it for the money.

—E.R.

A professor watched while a mechanic removed engine parts from his car to get to the valves. A surgeon, waiting for his car being repaired, walked over to observe the process. After they introduced themselves, they began talking and the talk turned to their lines of work.

"You know, doctor," the professor said, "I sometimes believe this type of work is as complicated as the work we do."

"Perhaps," the surgeon replied. "But let's see him do it while the engine is running."

You've Been an ER Doctor Too Long If . .

• you think there should be a CPT-4 code for "Too Stupid to Live."

• lost vibrators and lost condoms are so routine you don't even bother to gossip about them.

• you automatically hold your breath as you start the pelvic exam.

I consider myself an expert on love, sex,
and health. Without health you can
have very little of the other two.

—Barbara Cartland

THINGS TO SAY TO YOUR DOCTOR DURING A PELVIC EXAM

"Have you found that skinny person they say is inside me trying desperately to get out?"

"Watch that you don't undo my belly button or my behind might fall off."

◆

A psychiatrist ushered a new patient into his office and began their session. "Now tell me, what is it that you would like to discuss?" he asked.

"I've become obsessed with hoarding money."

"Ah . . . It may take many, many sessions, but I believe I can help you overcome this."

Doctors can be frustrating. You wait a month and a half for an appointment, and then the doctor says, "You should've come to see me sooner."

A nurse was leaving the hospital one evening when she found a doctor standing in front of a shredder with a piece of paper in his hand.

"Listen," said the doctor, "this is important and my assistant has left. Can you make this thing work?"

"Certainly," said the nurse. She turned the machine on, inserted the paper, and pressed the start button.

"Excellent, excellent!" said the doctor as his paper disappeared inside the machine. "I'll need five copies of that."

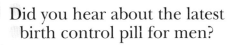

Did you hear about the latest
birth control pill for men?

You take it the day after.
It changes your blood type.

*I got well by talking. Death could not get a word in
edgewise, grew discouraged, and traveled on.*

—Louise Erdrich

The man looked a little worried when the doctor came in to administer his annual physical, so the first thing the doctor did was to ask whether anything was troubling him.

"Well, to tell the truth, Doc, yes," answered the patient. "You see, I seem to be getting forgetful. No, it's actually worse than that. I'm never sure I can remember where I put the car, or whether I answered a letter, or where I'm going, or what it is I'm going to do once I get there—if I get there. So I really need your help. What can I do?"

The doctor mused for only one or two beats, then answered in his kindliest tone, "Pay me in advance."

Apprehension, uncertainty, waiting, expectation, fear of surprise do a patient more harm than any exertion.

—Florence Nightingale

A motorcycle patrolman was rushed to the hospital with an inflamed appendix. The doctors operated and advised him that all was well. However, the patrolman kept feeling something pulling at the hairs on his chest. Worried and confused, he finally got enough energy to pull his hospital gown open so he could look at what was making him so uncomfortable. Three wide strips of adhesive tape were firmly affixed across his hairy chest. Written on them in large black letters was the sentence:

"Get well quick. And think twice before you give a nurse a speeding ticket."

How is a hospital gown like insurance?

You're never covered as much
as you think you are.

Patient: Jane Doe   Date: October 22, 2003   Time: 15:23
X-Ray of Pelvis area and lower back   Doctor I.M. Aquack

*Some people think that doctors and nurses can put
scrambled eggs back into the shell.*

—Dorothy Canfield Fisher

A man was rushed for emergency surgery to Mercy Hospital. His operation went well, and when he regained consciousness he found a Sister of Mercy sitting by his bed.

"You're going to be just fine," the nun said, patting his hand. "We do have to know, however, how you intend to pay for your treatment here. Are you covered by insurance?"

"No, I'm not," the man whispered hoarsely.

"Can you pay in cash?"

"I'm afraid I can't, Sister."

"Do you have any relatives who might help?"

"Just my sister in New Mexico, but she's a spinster nun."

"Nuns are not spinsters," the nun replied. "They are married to God."

"Well then," the man said with a smile, "I'm sure my brother-in-law will be willing to foot the bill."

How to Distinguish Medical School from Hell

• In hell some people still smile.

• You don't have to study organic chemistry to get into hell.

• Even in anger, you'd never tell a friend to go to medical school.

An expectant mother was being rushed to the hospital, but didn't quite make it. She gave birth to her baby on the hospital lawn. Later, the father received a bill listing "Delivery Room Fee: $500."

He wrote the hospital and reminded them the baby was born on the front lawn. A week passed, and a corrected bill arrived: "Greens Fee: $200."

Three paramedics were boasting about improvements in their ambulance teams' response times. "Since we installed our new satellite navigation system," bragged the first one, "we cut our emergency response time by 10 percent."

"Not bad," the second paramedic commented. "But by using a computer model of traffic patterns, we've cut our average ERT by 20 percent."

The third paramedic said, "That's nothing! Since our ambulance driver passed the bar exam, we've cut our emergency response time in half!"

◆

I've never understood the fear of some parents about babies getting mixed up in the hospital. What difference does it make as long as you get a good one?

—Heywood Brown

"I'm sorry," the dentist said to a patient. "I won't be able to see you this afternoon. I've got eighteen cavities to fill." Then he picked up his golf bag and headed for the door.

◆

Your body is the baggage you must carry through life. The more excess baggage the shorter the trip.

—Ellen Glasgow

STRANGE BUT TRUE MEDICAL STORIES

A customer complained to a pharmacist that the capsules he'd been given weren't working. "Oh," she said, "you've been taking them the wrong way. You have to take them so that the green half goes in first." The customer stopped by a week later to let her know that his medication was working fine now.

Medical Chart Bloopers

The chart of an Alzheimer's patient read,
"Patient very agitated yelling profound statements."
Profane? Yes. Profound? Doubtful.

A man asks his doctor what to do about his bad-smelling breath. The doctor examines him and says, "Either stop biting your nails or stop scratching your hemorrhoids."

A surgical patient was given the usual postoperative instructions. That night she called, wanting to know if her mother could visit.

"Any time," the doctor replied. "Why do you ask?"

"It says here in your instructions, 'no relations until after your post-op checkup.'"

A doctor in the obstetrics ward was checking on a young expectant mother who had come to the hospital for her delivery. "Is this your first baby?" the doctor asked.

"Yes," the mother-to-be answered calmly.

"Are you having any contractions or pressure?"

"No."

"Are you having any discomfort?"

"No."

The doctor was perplexed. "If you don't mind me asking," she said, "why are you here?"

"Because today is my due date!"

———◆◆◆———

Illness is a great leveler. At its touch, the artificial distinctions of society vanish away. People in a hospital are just people.

—M. Thorek

Nearing the end of a long, busy shift in the emergency room, a tired nurse leaned back against a counter and sighed. "Worn out?" asked the charge nurse.

"You got it. You know, at times like this I think I should have been a nun."

"A nun? What makes you say that?"

"Well," the weary nurse said, "here I have to answer to at least a dozen doctors, all night, every night. A nun only has to serve one God."

FROM ACTUAL MEDICAL RECORDS

She has no rigors or shaking chills, but her husband states she was very hot in bed last night.

A man working in a lumber mill accidentally sheared off all ten of his fingers. When he arrived at the emergency room, the doctor on duty said, "Yuck! Well, give me the fingers, and I'll see what I can do."

"I haven't got the fingers," the lumberman said.

"What do you mean, you haven't got the fingers?" the doctor cried. "We've got microsurgery and all sorts of other incredible techniques for just this type of situation. I could have put those fingers back on and made you like new. Why didn't you bring them with you?"

"Well, Doc, why don't you tell me how exactly I was supposed to pick 'em up."

A new study claims that mouth-to-mouth resuscitation is not necessary during CPR and it's better to skip right to chest compression. However, the study says that you're still required to snuggle for a half hour afterward.

—Conan O'Brien

Sign found in the lobby of a doctor's office:
PLEASE DO NOT REMOVE THE MAGAZINES
FROM THE OFFICE. THE NURSE WILL TELL YOU
HOW THE STORY ENDS.

Ways to Get Rid of Drug Reps

• Schedule four of them at the same time. Only see the one who emerges from your waiting room alive.

• Take the rep back to your office and confidentially tell him that you've had a bit of a problem with your DEA license. Could he provide you with lots of free samples?

• Get your information about psychopharmacology from talking to colleagues, attending seminars, and reading journals.

———————◆◆◆———————

The difficulty with becoming a patient is that as soon as you get horizontal, part of your being yearns, not for a doctor, but for a medicine man.

—Shana Alexander

An eighty-five-year-old man went to see his doctor. After a complete physical, the doctor told the man that if he gave up smoking and drinking, he might live to be 100. The old man climbed down from the examining table and gave his doctor a dirty look. "You call that living?" the old man said.

Surgeons must be very careful
When they take the knife!
Underneath their fine incisions
Stirs the Culprit—Life!

—Emily Dickinson

Autopsy FAQs *(from your friendly family pathologist)*

WILL IT HURT?
We certainly hope not. If at any time you're feeling uncomfortable, please feel free to alert the pathologist.

WHEN CAN I RETURN TO WORK?
Not for a while. We suggest you worry about this after your autopsy.

WILL I HAVE A SCAR?
We take vanity into consideration. You may have a large "Y" shaped incision on your torso. There may also be some scalp incisions that can be covered by a competent professional.

For further information, please refer to our brochures "Cadaver's Bill of Rights" and "So You're Dead. What Next?"

"I don't like what I'm hearing from your heart," the doctor said to the young man as she pulled back the stethoscope. "You've had some trouble with angina pectoris, haven't you?"

"You've got the right idea, doctor," the man said, blushing. "Only that isn't her name."

DOCTORS' SECRET HANDSHAKES

Cardiologist: *left hand on your wrist, feeling pulse*
Dermatologist: *wears a latex glove*
Gynecologist: *index and middle fingers extended*
Pediatrician: *thumb extended*
Psychiatrist: *grasps his own hand*

Just after midnight, there was a rapping at the doctor's door. He dragged himself from bed and poked his head out the window. Spotting a lone figure, he shouted down, "Well?"

"No," came the mournful reply, "sick."

A young man sidled up to a woman at a bar and asked, "What do you do?"

"I'm a doctor."

"I wish I could be ill and let you doctor me," he whispered in her ear.

"Be careful what you wish for," she replied. "I'm a proctologist."

TOP TEN SIGNS YOU'VE GONE TO A BAD CHIROPRACTOR

10. When you walk, you make a wacky accordion sound.

9. Keeps saying, "A spine is like a box of chocolates."

8. Repeatedly asks, "You a cop? You sure you ain't a cop?"

7. Over and over, you hear crunching sounds followed by "Uh-oh."

6. There's a two-drink minimum.

5. At end of session, lies down on the table and says, "My turn!"

4. He was nowhere near Woodstock and yet he's covered with mud.

3. Rushes in late to your appointment still wearing his Burger King uniform.

2. Hints that for an extra $50, he'll "straighten" something else.

1. You're fully clothed and he's naked.

—David Letterman

A man is talking to the family doctor. "Doc, I think my wife's going deaf."

The doctor answers, "Well, here's something you can try on her to test her hearing. Stand some distance away from her and ask her a question. If she doesn't answer, move a little closer and ask again. Keep repeating this until she answers. Then you'll be able to tell just how hard of hearing she really is."

The man goes home and tries it out. He walks in the door and says, "Honey, what's for dinner?" He doesn't hear an answer, so he moves closer to her. "Honey, what's for dinner?" Still no answer. He repeats this several times, until he's standing just a few feet away from her. Finally, she answers, "For the eleventh time, I said we're having meatloaf!"

Q. What is a double-blind study?

A. Two orthopedists reading an electrocardiogram.

A man's illness is his private territory and, no matter how much he loves you and how close you are, you stay an outsider. You are healthy.

—Lauren Bacall

STRANGE BUT TRUE MEDICAL FACTS

One out of every four patients diagnosed with high blood pressure in the doctor's office has normal blood pressure when measured away from the doctor's office.

A young man went into the hospital for some minor surgery. The day after the procedure, a friend stopped by to see how he was doing. The friend was amazed to find a veritable parade of female doctors and nurses coming in to check on him and tend to his every need.

"Why all the attention?" the friend asked. "You look fine to me."

"I know," said the patient. "It's been like this ever since I told a nurse that my circumcision required twenty-seven stitches . . ."

Medical Chart Bloopers

For Halloween, the Children's Hospital let each nursing unit decorate pumpkins using the unit's theme. They also let the kids decorate pumpkins and take them to their rooms. The kids were reluctant to part with the pumpkins, even though after a while they began to rot. Not realizing the source of the foul odor, one doctor came in and wrote an order to "bathe patient stat!"

———◆———

The doctor got the lab results back and telephoned his patient. "You're not in good shape at all, I'm afraid," he said. "The best thing for you to do would be to give up liquor, cut out the rich food from your diet, and stop staying out late."

"What's the next best thing?" the patient asked.

A distraught patient phoned her doctor's office. "Is it true," the woman wanted to know, "that the medication you prescribed has to be taken for the rest of my life?"

"Yes, I'm afraid so." The doctor told her.

There was a moment of silence before the woman continued, "I'm wondering, then, just how serious my condition is. This prescription is marked 'No Refills.'"

Q. What do physicians do when pharmaceutical salesmen knock on their doors?
A. Vitamin!

MEMO
To: All Doctors
Subject: Death

Other than your own: This is not an acceptable reason for missing work. The deceased party no longer requires your assistance.

Your own: Time off is allowed, provided you give at least two weeks prior notice.

You know you're a doctor when your twelve-year-old daughter in the back seat of the car asks, "Mom, what date was I due on?" and then proceeds to figure up on a stray gestational wheel when she was conceived.

Everyone who is born holds dual citizenship, in the kingdom of the well and in the kingdom of the sick. Although we all prefer to use only the good passport, sooner or later each of us is obliged, at least for a spell, to identify ourselves as citizens of that other place.

—Susan Sontag

TOP TEN ITEMS
in [former] President Clinton's Medical File

10. His small intestine mysteriously bears the "KFC" logo.

9. He's the first president with a double-jointed stomach.

8. Under "fat to muscle ratio," doctor wrote, "Like, about a zillion to one".

7. Since being elected, he's had three hysterical pregnancies.

6. Just lost twenty pounds through strict exercise regimen of constant sex.

5. Soreness in lower back from years of flip-flopping.

4. He's at the ideal weight for a man who is eight feet tall.

3. Pasty whiteness of thighs caused by layers of powdered donut sugar.

2. Slight abrasions on knees from climbing out of White House window at 3 A.M.

1. His blood type: A-1.

—David Letterman

A doctor found it easier to communicate with one of his elderly, hard-of-hearing patients by writing her notes. One day she came to the office for some test results. "Now, doctor" she said sternly, "if you have anything to tell me, please have your secretary type it. Frankly, your handwriting is worse than my hearing."

How many surgeons does it take
to change a lightbulb?

None. If you're having trouble with the bulb, it could
be the socket, which may cause you problems in
the future. Therefore, they will remove the socket.

Four hospital patients, bored and unable to secure playing cards, took the diagnoses from a nurse's pocket as she went by. They began a game of draw poker, and the first hand came down to two players.

"Beat this," said the first. "I have three appendices and two gallstones."

"I think I've got you," said the second. "I have four enemas."

"Okay," the first replied, "you win the pot."

◆

Patient: *Help me. I think I'm a bell.*

Doctor: *Take these and if it doesn't help, give me a ring.*

Two men were sitting in a free health clinic. One of the men couldn't help but notice that the other man was crying, so he put his hand on the tearful man's shoulder and asked what was the matter.

"I came here for a blood test," the crying man said.

"Are you afraid of the results?" the other man said.

"No, it's not that. I just know that to take my blood, they'll have to cut my finger."

Hearing that, the other man began to sob as well.

"Why are you crying?" asked the man in for the blood test.

"I'm here for a urine test," the other man said.

A new medical facility was opening in a trendy part of town. Wanting to be creative, the administration decided that each doctor's office door would, in some way, be representative of the practice performed inside. The ophthalmologist's door was given a peep hole; the orthopedist's door had a broken hinge; the psychiatrist's door was painted after the style of Jackson Pollock; and the proctologist's door was left open, just a crack.

Sickness, like sex, demands a private room, or at the very least, a discreet curtain around the ward bed.

—Violet Weingarten

On a particularly cold day, a well-bundled woman ran out of her apartment building and hailed a cab. "Quick! The maternity ward at City Hospital!" she said. Seeing the worried look on the cabby's face, she added, "Don't worry, pal. I'm just late for work."

A man goes to a doctor because of chest pains. The doctor says, "Well, there are two divergent opinions on how best to treat you. I'm convinced you need a triple bypass. Your HMO says all you need to do is rub this $14 tube of salve on your chest."

REAL ILLNESSES
(AND THEIR ACTUAL MEDICAL NAMES)

Humpers Lump: Swelling suffered by hotel porters from lugging heavy bags.

Ice Cream Frostbite: Frostbite on the lips from prolonged contact with ice cream.

Jeans Folliculitis: Irritation of the hair follicles from the waist down to the knees caused by ultratight jeans.

Q. Did you hear about the plastic surgeon
who sat too close to the fireplace?

A. He melted.

Show me a sane man and I will cure him for you.

—Carl Jung

As the patient was leaving the doctor's office, the doctor pulled his wife aside and said, "There's nothing wrong with your husband. He just thinks he's sick."

After a few days, the doctor called to check up on the patient. "How's your husband?" he asked.

"He's worse," said the wife. "Now he thinks he's dead."

A gastroenterologist has a perfect way to deal with patients who complain incessantly of nervous indigestion. He asks if his patients play golf. If they say, "Yes," he tells them to stop. If they say, "No," he recommends that they start.

The doctor entered the examining room and said, "I have some good news for you, Mrs. Douglas."

"Pardon me," she interrupted, "but it's Miss."

The doctor said, "I have some bad news for you, Miss Douglas."

Medical Chart Bloopers

"55 yr m admitted with signs of chest pain. Pleasant to speak with. Family aware of status. Patient states that chest pain occurred while his wife was on him having dinner. Cardiac protocol taken."

Found on doctor's orders for the same patient:
"Discontinue Viagra."

◆

Q. How many nurses does it take to change a lightbulb?

A. Five. One to change the bulb, one to check policy and procedure, one to document, one to maintain quality assurance, and one to represent the Task Force on Hospital Lighting.

A skilled nurse died and arrived before Saint Peter, who explained, "We have this little policy of allowing you to choose whether you want to spend eternity in heaven or in hell." "How do I know which to choose?" she asked.

"That's easy," said Saint Peter. "You have to spend a day in each place before making a decision." With that, he put the nurse on an elevator and sent her down to hell. The elevator doors opened and the nurse found herself in a sunny garden, where many former friends and colleagues warmly greeted her. She had a great time all day laughing and talking about old times. That night, she had an excellent supper in a fantastic restaurant. She even met the devil, who turned out to be a pretty nice guy. Before she knew it, her day in hell was over and she returned to heaven.

The day in heaven was okay. She lounged around on clouds, sang, and played the harp. At the end of the day,

Saint Peter came and asked for her decision. "Well, heaven was great and all," the nurse said, "but I had a better time in hell. I know it sounds strange, but I choose hell." With that, she got in the elevator and went back down.

When the doors opened, she saw a desolate wasteland covered in garbage and filth. Her friends, dressed in rags, were picking up garbage and putting it in sacks. When the devil walked over, she said to him, "I don't understand. Yesterday, this place was beautiful. We had a delicious meal and a wonderful time laughing and talking." The devil smiled and said, "Yesterday we were recruiting you. Today you're staff."

Two friends were having lunch together. The first one said, "That psychiatrist I've been seeing seems determined to diagnose me with some sort of neurosis."

"What makes you say that?" the friend replied.

"If I'm early for an appointment, she says I have an anxiety complex. If I'm late, I'm being hostile. And if I arrive on time, I'm being compulsive!"

One finger in the throat and one in the rectum makes a good diagnostician.

—Sir William Osler

Making rounds in the ICU, a doctor prepared to check on her partner's patient. The nurse whispered a warning. "He's the guy who owns the big Lexus dealership. And the lady in there isn't his daughter, it's his wife."

The patient seemed a bit confused. His color wasn't very good, his lungs were starting to fill up, and his blood pressure had been drifting downward. The doctor asked his wife to step outside the room. "I have to tell you, I don't like how your husband looks," the doctor said.

"Well, neither did I. But he's rich, and he's really good with the children."

◆

What the doctor says: I have some good news and some bad news.

What the doctor means: The good news is, I'm going to buy that new BMW. The bad news is, you're going to pay for it.

Strange but True Medical Stories

A drunk staggered into a Pennsylvania emergency room complaining of severe pain while trying to remove his contact lenses. He said that they would come out halfway, but they always popped back in. A nurse tried to help using a suction pump, but without success. Finally, a doctor examined him and discovered the man did not have his contact lenses in at all. He had been trying to rip out the membrane of his cornea.

It is more important to know what sort of person has a disease than to know what what sort of disease a person has.

—Hippocrates

After his wife had given birth to a baby girl, a panicked Japanese man went to see the obstetrician. "Doctor," he said, "I don't mind telling you, I'm very upset. My daughter has red hair. She can't possibly be mine."

"Nonsense," the doctor said. "You and your wife both have black hair, but one of your ancestors may have contributed red hair to the gene pool."

"Doctor, please be serious," the man said. "Both of our families are Asian through and through."

"Well . . ." said the doctor. "Let me ask you this. How often have you and your wife been having sex?"

"I've been working very hard for the past year. We only made love once or twice a month."

"Ah, there's your answer!" the doctor said. "It's just rust."

REAL ILLNESSES
(AND THEIR ACTUAL MEDICAL NAMES)

Birdwatchers Twitch: The nervous excitement of spotting a species for the first time.

Bodybuilders Psychosis: Psychotic episodes associated with the use of anabolic steroids, causing hallucinations, paranoid delusions, grandiose beliefs, and manic-depressive symptoms.

Strange but True Medical Stories

One day a doctor had to be the bearer of bad news and tell a wife that her husband had died of a massive myocardial infarct. Not more than five minutes later, he heard her reporting to the rest of the family that he had died of a "massive internal fart."

The plastic surgeon and his wife are walking on the beach when they find an old oil lamp. As they brush the sand from the lamp, a genie appears.

"You each may have one wish," the genie says.

"Well, I'm forty-five, and it's time I had what's due to me," says the wife. "I wish I lived in a ten-million-dollar mansion overlooking this beach." And—poof—she disappears, and a huge ornate building suddenly appears on the bluff.

"And you?" asks the genie.

"I'll tell you what I want," says the doctor. "I wish I was married to someone half my age." And—poof—he's suddenly ninety years old.

Mr. Smith called the doctor's office to find out his wife's test results. "I'm sorry," the nurse said, "but there's been a bit of a mix-up. When we sent your wife's samples to the lab, some samples from another Mrs. Smith were sent as well. One Mrs. Smith has tested positive for Alzheimer's disease and the other for AIDS. We can't tell which results are your wife's."

"That's terrible!" Mr. Smith cried. "Can we do the test over to see the right answer?"

"Normally, yes. But your HMO won't pay for these expensive tests to be run twice."

"Well, what are we supposed to do?"

"The doctor recommends that you drop your wife off in the middle of town. If she finds her way home, don't sleep with her."

REAL ILLNESSES
(AND THEIR ACTUAL MEDICAL NAMES)

Electronic Space-War Video-Game Epilepsy: Epilepsy caused by the flashing lights of electronic video games.

Espresso Wrist: Pain in espresso coffee machine operators from strong wrist motions required to make the coffee.

Flip-Flop Dermatitis: Skin disease on feet from wearing rubber flip-flops.

I have so little sex appeal,
my gynecologist calls me "sir."

—Joan Rivers

———◆———

An expectant father did not want his coworkers to know that he had a girlfriend, much less that she was pregnant with his son. Though he accompanied her to the hospital, he had to report to work while she was still in labor. As he left he asked the labor and delivery nurse to call his office and let him know by using a secret code.

"When my son comes, do not call up the office and say that I have become a father of a boy, otherwise everyone will know. Just tell the receptionist that the clock has arrived and I will know that my son has been born."

The child arrived but it was a girl. The labor and delivery nurse thought, "If I tell his office that the clock did not arrive, he'll think that something has happened to the baby and he'll be terribly upset and worried."

So she sent the message: "The clock has arrived, but the pendulum is missing."

———◆———

A worried father telephoned his family doctor and said that he was afraid that his teenage son had come down with V.D. "He says he hasn't had sex with anyone but the maid, so it has to be her."

"Don't worry too much," advised the doctor. "These things happen."

"I know, doctor," said the father, "but I have to admit that I've been sleeping with the maid also. I seem to have the same symptoms."

"That's unfortunate."

"Not only that, I think I've passed it to my wife."

"Oh God," said the doctor, "that means we all have it."

Top Ten Signs It's Cold and Flu Season in New York

10. Fake Rolex guys also selling fake Sudafed.

9. If you dial 911, you hear, "Everyone's out sick. Please call back in May".

8. To many feverish audience members, *Cats* is actually entertaining.

7. Mob corpses in East River are wearing scarves and mittens.

6. Hookers offering a $50 "Vapo-Rub" service.

5. Street vendors boiling their hot dogs in Thera-Flu.

4. Guy who rubs up against you in the subway also feels your forehead to see if it's hot.

3. Cab drivers wearing turbans made of used Kleenex.

2. Drug dealers selling "nighttime sniffling, sneezing, achy, stuffy-head, fever, so you can rest" crack.

1. Sound of sneezing drowns out gunfire.

—David Letterman

Strange But True Phobias

- Metrophobia is the fear of poetry.
- Peladophobia is the fear of bald people.
- Iatrophobia is the fear of going to the doctor.

A woman was rushed to the hospital unexpectedly, so she called her husband to bring her a few items from home. One item on her list was "comfortable underwear."

Not sure what she considered comfortable, he asked, "How will I know which ones to pick?"

"Hold them up and imagine them on me," she answered. "If you smile, put them back."

———◆———

You get very excited when they call you because you think now you're going to see the doctor. But you're not. You're going into the next, smaller waiting room. But now, you don't even have your magazine. You've got your pants around your ankles, you're sitting on that butcher paper they pull out over the table. Sometimes I bring a pickle with me and I put it next to me right there on the table. I don't know, in case the doctor wants to fold the whole thing up for a to-go order.

—Jerry Seinfeld

———◆———

FAVORITE CHRISTMAS CAROLS, BY PSYCHIATRIC DISORDER

Schizophrenia: "Do You Hear What I Hear?"

Multiple Personality Disorder: "We Three Kings Disoriented Are"

Dementia: "I Think I'll Be Home for Christmas"

A woman walked up to a little old man sitting on his porch. "I couldn't help noticing how happy you look," she said. "What's your secret for a long, happy life?"

"I smoke three packs of cigarettes a day," he replied. "I also drink a case of whiskey a week, eat fatty foods, and never exercise."

"That's amazing," the woman said. "How old are you?"

"Twenty-six."

STRANGE BUT TRUE PHOBIAS

• Pupaphobia is the fear of puppets.

• Syngenesophobia is the fear of relatives.

• Linonophobia is the fear of string.

◆

FAVORITE CHRISTMAS CAROLS, BY PSYCHIATRIC DISORDER

Narcissistic: "Hark! the Herald Angels Sing About Me"

Paranoid: "Santa Claus Is Coming to Get Me"

Borderline Personality Disorder: "Thoughts of Roasting on an Open Fire . . ."

———◆◆◆———

Three men—two nurses and one doctor—died on Christmas Eve and were met by Saint Peter at the pearly gates.

"In honor of the season," Saint Peter said, "you must each possess something that symbolizes Christmas to get into heaven on this holy day."

The first nurse fumbled through his pockets and pulled out a penlight. He flicked it on. "It represents a holy candle," he said.

"You may pass through the pearly gates," Saint Peter said.

The second nurse reached into his pocket and pulled out a set of keys. He shook them and said, "They're bells."

Saint Peter said, "You may pass through the pearly gates."

The doctor started searching desperately through his pockets and finally pulled out a pair of women's panties.

"What do these have to do with Christmas?" Saint Peter asked. The doctor replied, "They're Carol's."

———◆◆◆———

He that sinneth before his Maker, Let him fall into the hand of the physician.

—Ecclesiasticus

———◆◆◆———

A girl was assigned to write a paper for school on childbirth, so she asked her parents, "How was I born?"

"Well," her prudish father said, "the stork brought you."

"And how was my brother born?" she probed further.

"The stork brought him, too."

"How about you and Mommy?"

"The stork brought us, too, dear, and Grandma and Grandpa as well!" the father said, and gave his daughter a dismissive pat on the head.

When the girl handed in her paper several days later, the teacher was taken aback by the first sentence: "This report focuses on the unusual case of my family, which has never experienced a natural childbirth."

Nurse: How old are you?

Patient: None of your business.

Nurse: But we have to know your age for our records.

Patient: Well, first multiply twenty by two, then add ten. Got it?

Nurse: Yes.

Patient: Okay, now subtract fifty, and tell me, what do you get?

Nurse: Zero.

Patient: Right. And that is exactly the chance you have of me telling you my age.

◆

Have you heard about the new medication that is both an aphrodisiac and laxative?

It's called "Easy Come, Easy Go."

Patient: It's been a month since my last visit and I still feel miserable.

Doctor: Did you follow the instructions on the medicine I gave you?

Patient: I sure did. The bottle said "keep tightly closed."

REAL ILLNESSES
(AND THEIR ACTUAL MEDICAL NAMES)

Money Counters Cramp: Painful seizure of muscles from counting too much cash.

Motorway Blues: The sort of headaches noted by drivers on congested motorways.

Nuns Knee: Swelling of kneecap from repeated kneeling in prayer.

Newscaster Kent Brockman: At 3 P.M. Friday, local autocrat C. Montgomery Burns was shot following a tense confrontation at Town Hall. Burns was rushed to a nearby hospital where he was pronounced dead. He was then transferred to a better hospital where doctors upgraded his condition to alive.

—The Simpsons

Common Medical Research Phrases and Their Real Meanings

Phrase: The most reliable results are those obtained by Smith . . .

Meaning: Smith was my graduate assistant.

Doctors are whippersnappers in ironed white coats,
Who spy up your rectum and look down your throats,
And press you and poke you with sterilized tools,
And stab at solutions that pacify fools.
I used to revere them and do what they said
Till I learned what they learned on was already dead.

—Gilda Radner

◆

MOVIE MEDICINE

Mary Wilke (Diane Keaton): Don't psychoanalyze me. I pay a doctor for that.

Isaac Davis (Woody Allen): Hey, you call that guy that you talk to a doctor? I mean, you don't get suspicious when your analyst calls you at home at three in the morning and weeps into the telephone?

—Manhattan

Did you hear about the baby born
in the high-tech delivery room?
It was cordless!

A city doctor started a practice in the countryside. He once had to go to a farm to attend to a sick farmer who lived there. After a few house calls he stopped coming to the farm. The puzzled farmer finally phoned him to ask if there was a problem.

The doctor said, "No, it's your ducks at the entrance. . . Every time I enter the farm, they insult me!"

A woman asked the man seated next to her on the airplane what he did for a living.

"I'm a Naval surgeon," the man said.

"Goodness' sake!" the woman said. "How you doctors specialize these days!"

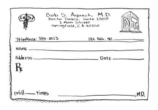

The Layman's Glossary of Medical Terms

D&C: The district in which the United States' capitol is located.

DILATE: To live a long life.

MOVIE MEDICINE

Ferris (Matthew Broderick): The key to faking out the parents is the clammy hands. It's a good nonspecific symptom. A lot of people will tell you that a phony fever is a dead lock, but if you get a nervous mother, you could land in the doctor's office. That's worse than school. What you do is, you fake a stomach cramp, and when you're bent over, moaning and wailing, you lick your palms. It's a little childish and stupid, but then, so is high school.

—Ferris Bueller's Day Off

Proctologist: *A doctor who puts in a hard day at the orifice.*

A physician is not angry at the intemperance of a mad patient, nor does he take it ill to be railed at by a man in a fever. Just so should a wise man treat all mankind, as a physician treats a patient, and look upon them only as sick and extravagant.

—Seneca

Suspecting a brain tumor, a doctor performed a spinal tap on a little old lady. During the painful procedure, the obviously distressed patient looked upward and whispered, "Help me. Please help me."

The specialist tried to soothe her by saying, "I'm sorry, but I'm doing the best I can."

Raising her head, the patient gave him a chilly stare and growled, "I wasn't talking to you."

TOP TEN SIGNS YOU'RE A BAD SURGEON GENERAL

10. You've got a pack of Marlboros rolled up in your lab coat sleeve.

9. You never appear in public without a half-empty bottle of Bacardi rum.

8. Morning, noon, and night, you can be found wandering around in a hospital gown.

7. Always confusing defibrillator with fry-o-lator.

6. You thought *Chicago Hope* was going to be a hit.

5. Your medical degree is from that correspondence school endorsed by Sally Struthers.

4. Instead of flu vaccine, you recommend so-called "flu-proof socks."

3. You smoke like a chimney and drink like a Kennedy.

2. You spend your entire day doing the very thing you said should be taught in school.

1. Your cure for heart disease: Zima.

—David Letterman

Two psychiatrists were at a convention. As they conversed over a drink, one asked, "What was your most difficult case?"

The other replied, "I had a patient who lived in a pure fantasy world. He believed that an uncle in South America was going to die and leave him a fortune. All day long he waited for a letter to arrive from an attorney. He never went out, he never did anything, he merely sat around and waited for this fantasy letter from this fantasy uncle. I worked with this man for eight years."

"What was the result?" the first doctor asked.

"It was an eight-year struggle, every day for eight years, but I finally cured him—and then that stupid letter arrived!"

———◆◆◆———

I once heard about a man who never drank and never smoked. He was healthy right up to the time he killed himself.

—Johnny Carson

Two very successful psychoanalysts occupied offices in the same building. One was forty years old, the other over seventy. They rode on the elevator together at the end of an unbearably hot, sticky day. The younger man was completely exhausted, and he noted with some resentment that his elder counterpart was as fresh as a daisy.

"I don't understand," he marveled. "How can you listen to drooling patients from morning till night on a day like this and still look so spry and unbothered when it's over?"

The older analyst said simply, "Who listens?"

———◆◆◆———

Did you hear about the three men who hijacked a truck full of Viagra?

The police are looking for a gang of hardened criminals.

Frequently Asked Questions about Managed Care

Question: My pharmacy plan covers only generic drugs. I need name brands because the generics upset my stomach. What can I do?

Answer: Give yourself a poke in the nose. That should take your mind off of your stomach ache.

You Might Be an ER Doctor If . . .

• You get an almost irresistible urge to stand and inhale your food as quickly as possible even in the nicest restaurants.

• You believe the waiting room should be equipped with a Valium fountain.

One has a greater sense of intellectual degradation after an interview with a doctor than from any human experience.

—Alice James

MOVIE MEDICINE

Hawkeye (Donald Sutherland): Beautiful. What do you think? Should we stop and play nine holes now and operate on the kid later? If he's still alive.

Trapper (Elliott Gould): I think we ought to operate first, no frills, get through it on the double. Then we'll be nice and relaxed on the course.

—M*A*S*H

Ever notice how dentists are incapable of asking questions that require a simple yes or no answer?

Stanford research group advertised for participants in a study of obsessive-compulsive disorder. They were looking for therapy clients who had been diagnosed with this disorder. The response was gratifying; they got 3,000 responses about three days after the ad came out. All from the same person.

Common Medical Research Phrases and Their Real Meanings

Phrase: It is believed that . . .

Meaning: I think.

MOVIE MEDICINE

Dr. Evil (Mike Meyers): It's Dr. Evil. I didn't spend six years in Evil Medical School to be called "mister," thank you very much.

—Austin Powers: International Man of Mystery

WASHINGTON—Hospitals cost almost 40 percent more in the United States than in Canada. . . . U.S. hospitals are more expensive, in part, because the cases they treat are 14 percent more complex. Dr. Donald Redelmeier, of Wellesley Hospital in Toronto, writing in the *New England Journal of Medicine* said this reflects social differences between the two countries. "Frostbite of the nose is not as expensive to treat as a shotgun wound to the belly," he said.

—The Vancouver Sun

A man leaned to the left because his left leg was shorter than his right. This leaning bothered the man's friend, until, finally, the friend recommended the man have his legs examined.

"Surgeons can fix your leg," the friend insisted.

"Nonsense," the man said.

For years, the friend told the man to see a doctor. Finally, the leaning man went to a surgeon who was able to make the man's legs the same length.

"What did I tell you?" the friend said to the man. "You didn't believe a doctor could fix your leg."

"You're right," the man said. "I stand corrected."

A young woman went to see her doctor for her regular check-up. After the doctor gave her a clean bill of health, he asked if she had any concerns.

"Well," the woman said, "there is one little thing."

"And what's that?" the doctor said.

"Well," the woman said, "every time I sneeze I have an orgasm."

"Oh my gosh," the doctor said. "What have you been taking for it?"

"Black pepper," she said.

◆

A lawyer who had been diagnosed with a weak heart went to see his doctor. "Give it to me straight, doc," the lawyer said. "How many billable hours do I have left?"

Did you hear about the patient who had the "clothing disease"? His tongue was coated and his breath came in short pants.

—Robert F. Early Sr., M.D., East Petersburg, Pennsylvania

This warning from the New York City Department of Health Fraud: *Be suspicious of any doctor who tries to take your temperature with his finger.*

—David Letterman

After an old man had undergone a successful surgery, his family was gathered at his bedside. When the old man regained consciousness, he told his family he wanted to get out of the hospital immediately. "I don't ever want to see another doctor again in my life," he told his son. "They're quacks."

"Dad, these doctors saved your life," the old man's son said. "Why do you say that?"

"Because I was in the operating room, and this anesthesiologist keeps telling me to breathe in and breathe out. Breathe in and breathe out, he says."

"So?" the son said.

"So I never went to college," the old man said. "But how else is a person supposed to breathe?"

—◆◆◆—

Medical students were seated in a lecture hall listening to a physician rail against the inherent dangers of alcohol. To prove his point, the doctor dropped a few worms into a jar filled with alcohol. In a few seconds, the worms were dead.

"Ladies and gentlemen, you can easily see the effect of liquor on lesser organisms," the doctor said. "What do you suppose this shows us about the effects of alcohol on humans?"

A student near the back raised his hand and said, "Anyone who drinks won't get worms."

The preservation of health is a duty.
Few seem conscious that there is
such a thing as physical morality.

—Herbert Spencer

—◆◆◆—

I'm a doctor, not a bricklayer!
I'm a doctor, not an escalator!
I'm a doctor, not a mechanic!
I'm a doctor, not an engineer!
I'm a doctor, not a coalminer!

—Dr. Leonard "Bones" McCoy, *Star Trek*

———◆◆◆———

A woman was having difficulty raising three small children by herself. When the children finally became too much for her, she went to her doctor complaining of severe migraines. The sympathetic physician handed the woman a bottle of pills. "Take three of these after lunch," the doctor said. "If you still have a headache by this evening, I want you to do what it says on the bottle."

"Take three every four hours?" the woman asked.

"No," the doctor said. "Keep out of reach of children."

Do you realize that somewhere in the world there exists a person who qualifies as the worst doctor? If you took the time, by process of elimination, you could actually determine the worst doctor in the world. And the nicest part is knowing that someone has an appointment to see him tomorrow.

—George Carlin

Patient: Doctor, doctor, I just don't understand it! I feel like a deck of cards. What's wrong with me?

Doctor: I've no idea. I'll deal with you later.

Patient: Doctor, should I file my nails?

Doctor: No, throw them away like everybody else.

An elderly woman was brought to the emergency room of a hospital after she had fractured her hip. The attending physician knew that surgery would be in order for the woman. "Have you ever undergone surgery?" the doctor asked.

"Yes," the woman said.

"What type of surgery was it?" the doctor said.

"I'm not sure," the old woman said. "It was a long time ago."

The doctor noticed a scar on the right side of the woman's abdomen. He pointed to the scar. "Is this where you had the surgery?" he asked.

"No," the woman said. "It was in Brooklyn."

PSYCHIATRY: *The care of the id by the odd.*

———◆◆◆———

Before I heard the doctor tell,
The dangers of a kiss,
I had considered kissing you
The nearest thing to bliss,
But now I know biology,
And sit and sigh and groan—
Six million mad bacteria!
I thought we were alone.

*Doctors said that the test most commonly used to
screen for colon cancer doesn't go far enough.
They're recommending a procedure that involves
photographing the entire colon. I say, don't
give CBS an idea for another reality show.*

—Bill Maher

———◆◆◆———

A nurse rushed into her doctor's private office. "Doctor!" the nurse said, "That Mr. Taylor you just gave a clean bill of health dropped dead outside the front door. What should I do?"

The doctor looked up from his paperwork. "Turn him around so it looks like he was coming in," he said. "Then call 911."

◆

A woman who had thrown a dinner party at which raw oysters, steak tartare, and steamed mussels were all served, met her physician on the street the following day. "I'm sorry you weren't able to come to my party last night," she said. "You're so busy these days, and I think it would have done you some good to have been there."

"Your party has done me good," he said. "I've just seen five of your dinner guests."

As a man, I do not like visiting our family doctor.
Like many general care practioners, he has a fancy
sheepskin diploma framed on the wall and a box of
latex gloves on the counter. The diploma apparently
authorizes him to use the gloves any way he sees fit.

—Bud Mortenson

A man went in for his annual physical and received a stellar bill of health from his doctor. "You're in great condition," said the doctor. "Is there anything else you need?"

"I was considering a vasectomy," the man said rather glumly.

"That's a big decision," the doctor said. "Have you discussed it with your family?"

"I have," the man said. "The vote was in favor 16-1."

A lawyer known for his frugality underwent a course of treatment for an obscure ailment.When he was well and received his bill, though, he was outraged. "My God," he said to his doctor. "That much for a week of treatments?"

"Listen," the doctor said. "If you knew how interesting your case was, and how tempted I was to let it run its course and go postmortem, you wouldn't complain one bit."

◆

Nineteen percent of doctors say that they'd be able to give their patients a lethal injection. But they also went on to say that the patient would have to be really, really behind on payments.

—Jay Leno

Four surgeons are on the golf course when there's a ringing sound. The first guy goes to his golf bag, pulls out his phone and talks for a minute. "Very important to be in touch these days," he says. Soon, another ring, and the second doctor holds his empty hand up to his head. "It's the latest in cell technology," he explains.

"A speaker's attached to my thumb, and a microphone to my pinky. You can't even see it."

Later, the third surgeon stands erect and begins talking. "This really is the latest. A speaker's implanted in my ear, and a microphone's in the back of a front tooth. I just stand at attention to talk." Suitably impressed, the foursome continues their game. Suddenly, the last surgeon excuses himself and ducks behind a bush. Finally, one of them goes to make sure he's okay. He finds him behind the bushes squatting down with his pants around his ankles. "If you could just give me a minute here," says the fourth surgeon, "I'm expecting a fax."

There once were some learned M.D.s
Who captured some germs of disease.
They infected a train,
Which, without causing pain,
Allowed one to catch it with ease.

MOVIE MEDICINE

*A harried medical receptionist: And here's
some brand-new information you've never
heard from this office: we are running late!
Now how could that happen . . . every day?*

—Dr T. & the Women

Have you heard about the new home surgery kit available through mail order?
It's called Suture Self.

"Doctor," Sylvia begs the psychiatrist, "you've got to help my husband. He thinks he's a racehorse. He wants to live in a stable, he walks on all fours—he even eats hay."

"I'm sure I can cure him," the shrink replies, "but it will take a long time and be very costly."

"Oh, money's no object," Sylvia says. "He's already won two races."

An elderly woman went to see her doctor. He examined her chart for a moment and said, "All right, Mrs. Jenkins, I'm going to ask you to get undressed."

"Oh, doctor, I don't know that you want to do that," Mrs. Jenkins said. "My husband died years ago."

"I'm sorry," the doctor said. "But I don't see what that has to do with anything. Please, get undressed."

"But doctor," Mrs. Jenkins said. "I've been living alone for the past fifteen years."

"Again, Mrs. Jenkins," the doctor said. "I don't see what that has to do with anything. If you'll get undressed, then we can begin."

"All right, doctor," Mrs. Jenkins said. "But I have to warn you. . . . You're playing with fire."

Hospitals are not places of exceptional etiquette. No one ever asks when you answer a page, "Did I get you at a bad moment? Is this a convenient time to talk?" Somehow the illusion is preserved that we are all sitting comfortably at big desks, telephones and notepads ready if we need them.

—Perri Klass, *Baby Doctor*

TRUE STORY

A man hobbled into the ER complaining of a permanent erection. He admitted to doctors that while on holiday in Cuba, he frequented many brothels, and in one he was given some erectile cream. He was told to use it sparingly. However, since he was having so much fun, he kept using more and more. By the time he came to the ER, all the blood vessels in his penis were swollen and his testicles had ballooned in size. Doctors could do nothing except prescribe pain killers, and told him that it would return to flaccidity in a few days. They also told him to enjoy his erection while it lasted, because it was going to be his last.

Rhinoplasty, that's what they call it. Rhinoplasty.
You've heard that term. Rhino. Is that necessary?
The person obviously is aware that there's a problem.
They made the appointment.

—Jerry Seinfeld

TRUE STORY

In Michigan, a man came into the ER with lacerations on his penis. He complained that his wife had "a rat in her vagina" that bit him during sex. After an examination of his wife, it was revealed that she had a surgical needle left inside her after a recent hysterectomy.

Doctor: I have the results of your amniocentesis here. Your blood count is perfect. Everything looks fine. . . .You have a normal, healthy, bisexual son. . . . [the happy couple turn to leave, but the husband stops in his tracks]

Husband: Wait. . . . I'm sorry, wait. You said, uh . . . bisexual?

Doctor: That's right.

Wife: How do you know? You know, about the bisexual part?

Doctor: Well, from the fetus's genetic code. . . .Your child— little Sammy—well, he'll be straight until he's in his mid-twenties . . . then he'll do some experimenting—it'll last for two years, just a phase, nothing to worry about.

Wife: You can tell that? That's incredible.

Doctor: Ma'am, we're doing things with genetics now that seemed impossible just twenty minutes ago.

—Saturday Night Live

A woman suffering from flu-like symptoms went to see her doctor. The waiting room was busy, however, and the woman spent two hours thumbing through magazines and staring at the walls before her name was called. She spent another half hour in the examining room before the doctor came in to see her.

"I'm very sorry you've had to wait so long," the doctor said.

"It's okay, doctor," she said. "But I wish you could have seen this problem in its early stages."

Anybody who goes to see a psychiatrist ought to have his head examined.

—Samuel Goldwyn

At a large British teaching hospital, an alcoholic was admitted for treatment. While making his rounds, the doctor asked the patient how he was feeling. According to Dr. Neil Carmichael of Newcastle under Lyme, England, the patient replied, "I must be missing the booze more than I expected, Doc. When I looked out the window, I thought I saw beer cans flying past."

Just then the doctor looked up and caught a glimpse of a beer can falling past the window. He did a little investigating and found a patient on the flocr above had a secret supply of beer hidden in his room. The upstairs patient had disposed of the empties by tossing them out of the window.

—Allan Zullo (with Martha Moffet), *Sick Humor: Outrageous but True Medical Stories from the ER to the OR*

———◆———

Three lunatics attempt an escape from a mental hospital. The first one passes the guard, makes a sound of a cat, and continues. The second one does exactly the same, meowing like a cat, and gets out, too. The third then passes near the guard and yells, "I'm a cat, too!"

You Might Be an ER Doctor If . . .

• Your next patient has maggots but isn't dead.
• You have writer's cramp and still have seven hours left on your shift.

———◆———

TRUE STORY

To boost morale, the dietary department often put inspirational messages on the patients' meal trays. Messages like "Have a nice day!" or "Smile!" accompanied meals. One day the message "Go crazy!" was placed on the psychiatric patient's dinner tray.

◆

I have come to appreciate what doctors bring to the bedside. Not only skills and training, but also our very lives and needs. The challenge, we suddenly realize, is to give back to our patients more than we receive. And we know that we can succeed only by fostering in ourselves a deep sense of purpose and by sharing whatever blessings we find along the way.

—David Loxterkamp, M.D., *A Measure of My Day: The Journal of a Country Doctor*

One of the first duties of the physician is to educate the masses not to take medicine.

—Sir William Osler

A new nurse at a hospital was perplexed by Dr. Warren's behavior. Off and on throughout her shift, Dr. Warren would run up and down the hall, yelling, "Typhoid, tetanus, measles!"

Finally, the new nurse asked the head nurse, "Why does Dr. Warren keep doing that?"

"Oh, just ignore him," the head nurse said. "He thinks he calls all the shots around here."

———◆◆◆———

MOVIE MEDICINE

James Bond (Peter Sellers): You can't shoot me! I have a very low threshold of death. My doctor says I can't have bullets enter my body at any time.

—Casino Royale

A man was brought into a hospital emergency room. He was unconscious and barely breathing, and while doctors worked to resuscitate the man, they looked to see if they could find any identification, such as a medical alert bracelet. They went through his wallet and pockets, but came up with nothing. Finally, one of them tugged at a chain around the man's neck. Attached to the end of the chain was a tag that read: *"If you read this while I am unconscious, do not give me any medication. I am drunk."*

———◆◆◆———

A young lawyer was attending the funeral of his former boss, the director of a hospital billing service. Another lawyer who worked for the same corporation arrived late. He slid into the pew behind the first lawyer and whispered,

"Where are they in the service?"

The first lawyer gestured toward the minister and replied, "He's just opening for the defense."

The doctor is to be feared more than the disease.

—Latin proverb

THE LAYMAN'S GLOSSERY OF MEDICAL TERMS

ENEMA: A person considered unfriendly, mean-spirited, and sometimes dangerous.

TABLET: A small article of furniture supported by legs and having a horizontal surface.

The patient asked his doctor, "So Doc, how did you happen to become a podiatrist?"

"Well," the doctor said. "I was at the foot of my class in school, so I just sort of walked right into the profession."

When an old general practitioner and his attractive nurse arrived at the hotel for a medical conference, they were somewhat disconcerted to find that instead of two single rooms, they had been booked into one twin-bedded room. There were no other rooms available, so they had to make do with what had befallen them.

That night, the old doctor flung the windows open for some fresh air and climbed into bed. After a short while, the nurse announced she was cold, and would he please close the windows.

The doctor said, "If you're cold, would you like to pretend we're married?"

The nurse giggled and said, "Why, doctor, what an idea, but I don't mind if that's what you'd like."

"Well, then, you get up and close the blasted window!"

Patient: I feel awful. I feel like a spoon all the time.
Doctor: Sit still and don't stir.

Patient: Can I have a second opinion?
Doctor: Sure. Come back tomorrow.

Frequently Asked Questions about Managed Care

Question: What if I'm away from home and I get sick?
Answer: Don't do that. You'll have a hard time seeing your primary care physician when you're 400 miles away from home. We recommend that you wait until you return from your trip, then get sick.

The United States physicist Dr. Robert Andrews Milliken was the first to measure the charge of an electron. He won the Nobel Prize in 1923. Dr. Milliken's wife once overheard their maid answering the phone. "Yes, this is where Dr. Robert Milliken lives," the maid said. "But he's not the kind of doctor who does anybody any good."

My illness is due to my doctor's insistence that I drink milk, a whitish fluid they force down helpless babies.

—W.C. Fields

◆

A priest, an ophthalmologist, and the CEO of an HMO prepared to tee off at a country club. However, they couldn't begin their game because players in front of them were hitting balls in all directions or missing shots entirely. They complained to the club pro.

"Relax," the pro said. "They were firefighters who lost their vision putting out a blaze we had at the club. We let them play for free."

"I feel terrible," the priest said. "I will pray for them."

"I feel awful, too," the ophthalmologist said. "I'll see if I can't get my colleagues to help them."

And the HMO CEO said, "Why can't these guys just play at night?"

An old man is visiting the emergency room. "What seems to be the problem?" he's asked.

"I can't pee any more!"

"Well, how old are you?"

"I am eighty-two years old."

"Well then, sir, you have peed enough."

A man's health can be judged by which he takes two at a time—pills or stairs.

—Joan Welsh

Patient: I think I've broken my neck!
Doctor: Don't worry, keep your chin up.

A physician was driving his son to a violin lesson when they had to stop and wait for a funeral procession to pass. The boy had never seen so many cars all in a line with their headlights on during the day.

"What is it?" the boy asked his father.

"That," the doctor said, "is a mistaken diagnosis."

TRUE STORY

A young woman with severe abdominal pains was rushed to a California emergency room. The attending physician asked her if she was sexually active. She said no. A later exam showed that she was pregnant. The doctor asked her why she said that she wasn't sexually active.

She replied, "I'm not. I just lie there."

The doctor then asked if she knew who the father was. "No. Who?" she asked.

The Thomases were shown into the dentist's office, where Mr. Thomas made it clear he was in a big hurry.

"No fancy stuff, doctor," he ordered. "No gas or needles or any of that stuff. Just pull the tooth and get it over with."

"I wish more of my patients were as stoic as you," said the dentist admiringly. "Now, which tooth is it?"

Mr. Thomas turned to his wife, Sue. "Show him your tooth, honey."

◆

The doctor stepped back from her patient. She scratched her head and said, "I'm not quite sure I can tell what's wrong with you, Mr. Lush. I'm afraid it's too much to drink."

"I understand, Doc," the patient said. "I'll just come back when you're sober."

A middle-aged woman has a heart attack and is taken to the hospital. While on the operating table she has a near-death experience. During that experience she sees God and asks if this is it. God says no and explains that she has another thirty years to live. Upon her recovery she decides to stay in the hospital and have a face lift, liposuction, breast augmentation, and a tummy tuck. She figures since she's got another thirty years, she might as well make the most of it. She walks out of the hospital after the last operation and is killed by an ambulance speeding up to the hospital. She arrives in front of God and complains: "I thought you said I had another thirty years."

God replies, "I didn't recognize you."

Dr. Ronald G. Worland of Medford, Oregon, reported that one of his colleagues wanted a patient to consult an ophthalmologist. The doctor suggested a specialist, but the patient shook her head. "I don't care to go to a doctor who advertises," she explained.

The physician made another recommendation, but once again, she declined, saying, "He advertises too."

The doctor came up with a third name. "I don't want to see him either, " she stated.

"Why not?" asked the now exasperated doctor.

"Because," she answered, "I never heard of him."

—Allan Zullo (with Martha Moffet), *Sick Humor: Outrageous but True Medical Stories from the ER to the OR*

An ophthalmologist belonged to a nine-member physician group. Each time any member of the group performed cataract surgery on a patient, they presented the patient with a T-shirt, which included the group name on the front and a print of a huge eye on the back.

One day, the ophthalmologist walked into an examination room to speak with an elderly patient on whom one of the other group members had performed cataract surgery. The woman was sporting her new T-shirt, which included the oversize eyeball on the back.

"I like your T-shirt," the doctor said.

"Yes," the woman said. "Thank goodness you guys aren't gynecologists."

You Might Be an ER Doctor If . . .

• The psychiatric patient who thinks he is Jesus is placed in the same room as another patient who thinks he is Satan.

• The psychiatric patient's delusions are starting to make sense.

A pharmaceutical salesman was received by a cynical physician in the physician's office. At the conclusion of the salesman's dubious pitch, he told the doctor, "I'd like to add, as long as I've represented this drug, our company has received no complaints."

The doctor leaned back in his chair and put his hands behind his head. "I guess dead men tell no tales," he said.

◆

A general medical officer in the U.S. Army was examining a young soldier with symptoms of a sexually transmitted disease. She routinely asked the young soldier if he had a discharge. He brightly answered, "Oh, no Ma'am! I have two more years."

Dr. Philip R. Alper of Burlingame, California, treated a seventy-eight-year-old patient named Victor for prostatitis and then billed Medicare accordingly.

Mystifyingly, Medicare wrote back, asking whether Victor was male or female. Dr. Alper's secretary answered that even if Victor's name wasn't a clue to his sex, the diagnosis certainly was. Incredibly, the secretary's letter did little good. After three months, the claim was still unpaid.

So Victor took matters into his own hands. He wrote to Medicare and threatened to send a nude photo with a frontal view of himself to prove that he was a male.

In no time at all, Medicare sent the check.

—Allan Zullo (with Martha Moffet), *Sick Humor: Outrageous but True Medical Stories from the ER to the OR*

Did you hear about the guy who had to undergo major stomach surgery? When they opened him up, out flew a flock of butterflies. The surgeon took a step back and scratched his head. "I'll be darned," he exclaimed. "The guy was right!"

Homer Simpson [to Bart]: I always knew you had personality. The doctor said it was hyperactivity, but I knew better.

—The Simpsons

———◆◆◆———

A gas station attendant came into the owner's office and said, "There's this guy out there, and he's got a flat tire. I told him we're real busy and can maybe get to it later in the day. He says I should fix it right now because he's your doctor. What do you want me to do?"

"You say he's got a flat?" the owner said.

"That's right," the young man said.

"Diagnose it as flatulency of the perimeter," the owner said. "And charge him way too much money. I'm sure he'll understand."

Common Medical Research Phrases and Their Real Meanings

Phrase: These results will be shown in a subsequent report . . .

Meaning: I'll get around to it later if I'm pushed.

———◆◆◆———

Leonard desperately wanted to become a doctor and had really crammed for his medical boards, so he wasn't in the least fazed by the question: "Name the three advantages of breast milk."

Quickly he wrote:

1. It contains the optimum balance of nutrients for the newborn child.

2. As it is contained within the mother's body, it is protected from germs and helps develop the child's immune system.

Then Leonard was stumped. Sitting back and racking his brain until he'd broken into a sweat, he finally scribbled:

3. It comes in such nice containers.

Three doctors were on their way to a medical convention when the car they were traveling in had a flat.

The three stepped out of the car and began to examine the tire.

"I think it's flat," the first doctor said.

"It sure looks flat," the second doctor said.

"It sure feels flat," the third doctor said.

The three stood, scratching their heads and wondering what they should do, until, in unison, they said,

"We'd better run some tests."

*A successful doctor is one who makes
enough money to be able to tell a
patient there's nothing wrong with him.*

—Joey Adams